P9-DFJ-269

Roland-Warne
Rowland

DATE DUE

JN 7 '93	AG 14 '98	
MY 27 '92	MAR 2 0 1999	
AUG 1 2 1992	OCT 2 4 2001	
OCT 2 4 1993		
OC 3 0 '93		
DE1 3 '93		
FE1 6 '94		
OCT 2 4 1994		
[OCT] 9 1995		
MAY 3 1997		

DEMCO

COSTUME

Early 19th-century beaded bag with hunting scene

Silk and velvet hat trimmings from the early 20th century

Late 19th-century circular fan

Boy's tunic dress from the early 19th century

Lady's late 19th-century silk bustle dress

Mid to late 19th-century silk and lace carriage parasol

Glass necklace from
the 1920s

1930s dress clips and bracelets

EYEWITNESS BOOKS

COSTUME

Written by
L. ROWLAND-WARNE

Women's red
leather gloves
from the 1940s

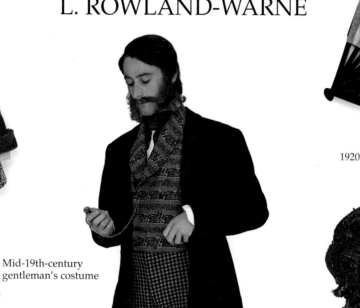

Mid-19th-century
gentleman's costume

1920s paper fan

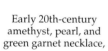

Early 20th-century
amethyst, pearl, and
green garnet necklace,

Ladies' evening turban
hat, 1913–1919

19th-century snuff
boxes

ALFRED A. KNOPF • NEW YORK

Viking shoe,
c. 900 A.D.

Girl's woolen coat
from the 1890s

A 1920s sporting
gentleman

Girl's cotton bonnet,
early 20th century

DK

A DORLING KINDERSLEY BOOK

Project editor Linda Martin
Art editors Michele Walker and Ann Cannings
Senior editor Helen Parker
Senior art editor Julia Harris
Production Louise Barratt
Picture research Cynthia Hole
Special photography Liz McAulay
Contributing writers Amy de la Haye (pp. 34/35,
56/57, 58/59, 62/63) and Margaret Mulvihill (pp. 8/9,
10/11, 12/13)
Consultant Ann Wise

C6-92

This Eyewitness Book has been conceived by Dorling
Kindersley Limited and Editions Gallimard

First American edition, 1992

Manufactured in Singapore
0 9 8 7 6 5 4 3 2 1

Library of Congress Cataloging in Publication Data
Rowland-Warne, L.
Costume / written by L. Rowland-Warne.
p. cm. — (Eyewitness books)
Includes index.
Summary: Photographs and text document the history
and meaning of clothing, from loincloths to modern
children's clothes.
1. Costume—Juvenile literature. 2. Costume—Pictorial
works—Juvenile literature. [1. Costume—History. 2.
Fashion—History.] I. Title.
GT518.R68 1992 391—dc20 91-53135
ISBN 0-679-81680-1
ISBN 0-679-91680-6 (lib. bdg.)

Color reproduction by Colourscan, Singapore
Printed in Singapore by Toppan

1920s umbrella and
snakeskin handbag

Late 19th-century
crocheted purse

Boy's jacket and vest
from the 1860s

17th-century flatiron

Contents

1940s children's hairslide and brooch

Early 20th-century children's socks, gloves, stockings, and boots

6
Why bother with clothes?
8
Cool and simple
10
Fabulous finery
12
Warm tunics and cloaks
14
Pointed hats and shoes
16
Rich, flowing, and heavy!
18
Bits and pieces
20
Slashes galore
22
Bells and boxes
24
Fancy feet
26
Ribbons and bows
28
A flourish of curls
30
Silk and brocade
32
Powder and patches
34
Bathing beauties
36
This and that
38
Cotton for all

40
The sewing machine
42
The cage of freedom
44
Blushing brides
46
Handy hats
48
Feathers and lace
50
A simpler line
52
A new world
54
Fashion foundations
56
Before and after
58
Minis, boots, and bell-bottoms
60
Boys and girls together
62
Fashion design
64
Index

Why bother with clothes?

CLOTHES HAVE BEEN WORN in one form or another for many thousands of years. The most influential factor leading to their "invention" was the need of early people to protect themselves against the climate, whether hot, cold, wet, or dry. For example, Ice Age cave dwellers wore animal skins for extra warmth, as some Inuit (Eskimo) people still do, while many native African people wore, and still wear, very little. Clothes are also used as a form of communication. Specialized clothing such as the regulation uniforms of police, soldiers, and nurses signifies status and position within society. Highly individual styles of dress, as adopted by teddy boys (pp. 56–57), hippies (pp. 58–59), and punk rockers (pp.58–59), make powerful and immediate statements about the wearer's lifestyle and beliefs. And then, of course, there is the question of modesty. In most societies, at least some clothing is worn in public. Clothes cover up the body at times when nakedness would be unacceptable.

MODESTY PREVAILS
The Bible tells us that it was only after Adam and Eve had eaten the apple that they became aware of their nudity and covered themselves with fig leaves.

Portrait of Kee-O-Kuk (Running Fox) by George Catlin, 1830

FEATHERS, FUR, AND BEADS
North American Indians wore highly decorated clothes: feathers, fur, and beads were all frequently used to add interest to their buffalo-skin costumes (pp. 38–39).

SECOND SKIN
The wearing of animal skins as protection against the cold dates back to about 30,000 years ago (during the Ice Age). Fur has been used for clothing in various forms ever since. Animal skins are still worn today, although concern about cruelty to animals and endangered species has reduced their popularity.

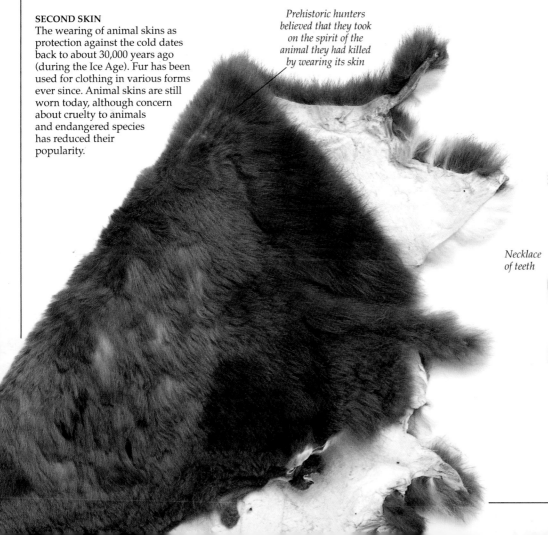

Prehistoric hunters believed that they took on the spirit of the animal they had killed by wearing its skin

Necklace of teeth

SKIN AND TEETH
Cave dwellers first tied and wrapped animal skins around themselves, but later learned to fit the skins to their bodies with stitching or by twisting the skins together. Hunters also wore the teeth of their dangerous victims as necklaces.

NOT A LOT
Aborigines have lived in Australia for at least 40,000 years, and maybe for much longer. Because of the hot climate in the south, their early dress consisted of waistbands, ornaments, and very little else. In colder northern areas, some wore cloaks of kangaroo and other fur.

SPINNING AND WEAVING
This woman is spinning the raw wool on the tree into a single thread by winding it around the spindle in her left hand.

BARK CLOTH *below*
Some of the earliest cloth was made by matting, or packing down, and pounding bark. The bark was soaked in water and pounded until it was soft. It was then oiled and painted before being draped around the body.

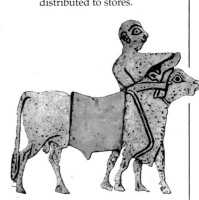

Mulberry bark was often used to make "tapa," or bark cloth

The color of most wool ranges from white to dark ivory. Darker wool has to be bleached before it can be dyed

WARM WOOL
Wool has been used to make clothes for about 10,000 years by peoples in small settled communities with land to graze sheep. Fleece like this was clipped off by methods very similar to those used today. The wool was then spun and the thread woven into cloth on a loom (top right).

MODERN PRODUCTION
Today's mass-production lines have made "fashion" readily available. Mass-produced clothing is manufactured in factories like the one above and widely distributed to stores.

Flounces of tufted wool

SUMERIAN SKIRTS
The transition from animal skins to woven cloth was not immediate. In between came the skirts and shawls made of tufted wool worn by the ancient Sumerian civilizations of Mesopotamia, c. 2900–2685 B.C. These skirts and shawls were built up of twisted tufts of wool or flax arranged in flounces, or wide ruffles, as seen in this detail of a Sumerian king.

Cool and simple

Such clothes as the ancient Egyptians wore were light and scanty, and made of linen, a material woven from the flax plant. Most of the time they wore very little. A slave's garment was as simple and rough as its wearer's daily life: loincloths for men, sheath dresses for women. To stay clean, cool, and comfortable, important Egyptians – such as members of the royal family, or priests – draped their bodies in very fine, veil-like linen. Linen was also highly prized in ancient Greece, where the women were also expert spinners and weavers of woolen cloth. Both materials were used to make the draped tunic-like garment worn by the ancient Greeks.

These bewigged diners wear robes of see-through linen. Their slaves are almost naked.

EVERYDAY UNIFORM
This basket-carrying figure shows a typical female costume of ancient Egypt. Such a tight-fitting dress would have been made from a single length of linen. The wide shoulder straps, instead of sleeves, left the arms free for work.

CROWNING GLORY *left*
When they dressed up, the Egyptians liked to wear wigs over their shaved heads. These wigs were made of human hair, flax, or palm fiber. They stayed on with the help of beeswax.

Long wigs were worn by wealthy Egyptians. Commoners wore a shorter "bob" style.

A PRIESTLY CUFF
Over centuries, the shape of basic garments stayed the same, but the decorative details changed. This surviving tapestry fragment was sewn onto the cuff of an Egyptian priest of about 700 B.C.

SCENTED FEET
For sandals the Egyptians used papyrus and other reeds, while the Greeks used leather. This ancient Greek perfume bottle is in the shape of a particularly delicate sandal.

WIG PINS
Apart from keeping elaborate hairstyles intact, long pins like these were used to fix cone-shaped pomades (knobs of perfumed ointment) in place on top of wigs. The fragrant grease gradually melted into the hair.

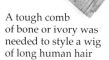

A tough comb of bone or ivory was needed to style a wig of long human hair

ONE SIZE
The peplos was a tubular garment folded over at the top and fastened at the shoulder with pins. The linen chiton, which gradually replaced it, was worn knee-length by men and full length by women.

Peplos

Chiton

PEPLOS PINS
These bronze pins held a peplos in place. According to the historian Herodotus, the peplos was replaced by the pinless chiton after a soldier was stabbed to death by women using their dress pins.

BRONZE HELMET
When not in use, a typical Greek helmet like this was simply pushed back on the head.

STEPPING OUT
Over her linen chiton a Greek woman wore a warm wrap called a himation, which was like a huge scarf. This outer garment was also worn by men. Sometimes hats like this little straw one were worn outdoors.

OLD AND NEW
The draped costume of this Kenyan girl would not have been unfamiliar in ancient Egypt or Greece, but the cotton fabric and its vibrant printed pattern would have caused quite a stir!

WATERBEARERS
These Greek women are modeling versatile chitons. With the aid of cords or belts around the waist, the full tunics could be separated to resemble blouses and skirts. A reddish-brown dye was popular among the common people, and embroidered borders gave an individual touch to basic outfits.

Fabulous finery

THE TOGA IS USUALLY thought to be the main garment of Roman costume, but in fact the most popular article of clothing was the tunic. Made of wool or linen, and to varying lengths, tunic dresses were worn by almost everyone. Roman women took great pride in their elaborate hairdos, but men were generally short-haired and clean-shaven. Baldness, however, was not admired: it was considered a deformity. In Rome's early days the citizens took pride in plain dressing. But as the Roman empire spread so did the extravagance. In A.D. 330, the emperor Constantine made Byzantium (now Istanbul) the empire's new capital. Its citizens enjoyed luxuries from all over Europe, cottons from India, and silk from China. Their clothes were colorful and lavishly trimmed.

FINGER RINGS
The Romans loved jewelry. Rings – of gold, jet, or other precious materials – were worn by both sexes, sometimes several on the same finger.

c. 200 B.C.

c. A.D. 100

c. A.D. 300

A RESPECTABLE CITIZEN
The toga, worn over a tunic, was the mark of Roman citizenship. The women's equivalent, the palla, was a large woolen shawl. By the time of the empire, togas were worn only on important occasions. Togas of magistrates and other officials had purple bands.

WEARING A TOGA
Over hundreds of years, the size and style of togas varied considerably. The early toga was quite simple and was worn with both ends thrown over the left shoulder (far left). The size and amount of decoration gradually increased, as shown in the middle picture. After the beginning of the second century, long and elaborately draped togas were worn, but only on ceremonial occasions.

Hobnailed sandal with an upper and sole

HEAVY-DUTY SANDALS
In hot areas of the empire, sandals protected the feet and kept them cool. But in northern Europe, warmth was important. These Roman sandals were found in London in the 1930s. Their dark color comes from the oil used to preserve them.

Sandal made from one piece of leather

SCULPTED LOCKS
Roman women liked complicated hairdos. A fashionable lady would spend hours having her locks sculpted by a hairdresser, the "ornatrix." Even hair color could be changed. Red and black dyes were available, while bleach was used for blond effects.

BYZANTINE SILK
The Byzantine love of finery was expressed in a fondness for silk, the finest of all natural fibers. Colored silk, woven with gold and silver threads, was especially prized. This preserved fringed fragment of Byzantine silk was originally purple and gold.

HAIR SCAFFOLDING
Imperial ladies' hairdos frequently involved rows of curls, waves, braids, and ringlets, as well as extra hairpieces, wigs, and tiaras. To hold such complicated styles in place, pins like these – made of bone or copper alloy – were used.

SILK WORKERS
Silkworm farming was big business in China, where all Byzantium's silk initially came from. Byzantium's silk industry began when two monks, acting on orders from Empress Theodora, returned from China with silkworm eggs hidden in a hollow cane.

GLAMOUR AND GLITTER
The Byzantine imperial family set the pace for style. From the top of her gem-encrusted crown, dripping with strings of pearls, to the tips of her embroidered slippers, the sixth-century empress Theodora (second from left) is a wonderful spectacle.

Warm tunics and cloaks

THE NORTHERN PEOPLE of Europe, the "barbarians," lived in colder, wetter conditions than did the people of the Mediterranean world, so they needed to wear layers of warm and relatively close-fitting clothes. Celtic, Teutonic, Anglo-Saxon, and Viking men wore woolen trousers of various styles. Sometimes these were long and loose, or they were strapped onto the lower leg by bandages of linen or by leather thongs. A typical barbarian wardrobe consisted of undertunic, shirt, trousers, overtunic, and cloak. Cloaks, tunics, gowns, nightgowns, boots, and mittens were often fur lined– or edged with fur. The women did not wear trousers, but under their long tunics they sometimes wore leg coverings that were made of wool or linen. When it came to decorative details, individual cultures had distinctive styles. The Celts liked abstract patterns, while the Anglo-Saxons were especially fond of animal designs.

A ROMANTIC GAUL
To the Romans, the barbarians were noisy, hairy, messy, and trousered. This romanticized picture of a French Celt (a Gaul) shows the kind of bronze helmets Celtic warriors liked to wear – often with horns or animal figures sticking out of them. These strange helmets gave courage to their wearers and terrified the enemy.

PORCUPINES
Although this 19th-century picture of Crusaders versus Saracens, nomadic Arab peoples, is not accurate – the Muslim armies did not fight in draped robes – it does show Norman knights wearing suits of interlinked metal rings known as chain mail. After a battle, knights embedded with enemy arrows were said to look like porcupines.

WINTER VIKING
A rank-and-file Viking wore trousers, a long-sleeved shirt, and a belted tunic. If he wore a woolen cloak rather than a fur wrap, it was fastened to his tunic by a brooch on his right shoulder (pp. 18–19). In case of action, it was important to leave the sword arm free. This Viking is wearing a simple helmet, but he might well have been wearing a snugly fitting hat made of leather, wool, or fur.

GILDED CHAIN
It is thought that this delicate chain of gilded copper alloy may have been a Saxon woman's girdle or belt. As a mark of her authority over a household, a Viking woman wore her keys on a chain hanging from her girdle or from one of her shoulder brooches.

Pendant is decorated with a crouching lion design

Charlemagne, king of the Franks from A.D. 768–814

Hand spindle for wool

Bone thread-pickers from Viking loom

PICTURE-BOOK VIKING
Real Vikings did not wear horned helmets like this one, but they did have armlets. Instead of paying wages, leaders often rewarded their followers with bracelets.

CHARLEMAGNE
This picture shows Charlemagne in his grand robes when he was crowned emperor of the Holy Roman Empire in A.D. 800. His day-to-day outfit would have consisted of tunics over trousers, a short, fur-lined cloak, and a round cloth cap.

WOMEN'S WORK!
No household was complete without the basic tools for spinning and weaving textiles, not just for clothes but also for sails, sacks, wall hangings, and bedding.

BONE AND ANTLER
These Viking combs, one of which has a fitted case (left), were highly crafted. The "teeth," carved into plates of bone, were clamped together by two riveted bars of red deer antler.

ALFRED THE GREAT
This statue gives us some idea of how the Saxon king of Wessex, England, looked. He probably had colorful clothes (dyed with vegetable juices). Otherwise, there was little difference between Anglo-Saxon and Viking dress.

BELT AND BROOCHES
These two beautifully decorated brooches were used by a barbarian to fasten his heavy cloak. The buckle and buckle plate are from a leather belt. Kings or nobles might have silver or gold brooches and buckles, but most people had bronze, copper, or even lead versions.

Belt buckle

Buckle plate

Pointed hats and shoes

B ECAUSE VERY FEW GARMENTS SURVIVE from the period before the 16th century, we have to rely on paintings and manuscripts to show us what people wore during the Middle Ages. Fortunately, these pictures are extremely detailed and reveal very precisely the fashions of the times. Europe was in the grip of feudalism; the privilege and power of the aristocracy is reflected in the exaggerated styles that originated at the Burgundian court in France, with rich, trailing garments and elaborate headdresses for women, and short tunics with wide sleeves and long, pointed shoes for the men. The peasants, meanwhile, were spinning and weaving their own fabrics in colorful designs. English and French merchants, Crusaders (above), pilgrims, and scholars all brought back exotic fabrics and styles from the Far East, Spain, and Italy, as well as from the Turks and Mongols.

Padded roll worn over a hairnet

Coils of hair enclosed in "templers" above each ear

Veil over horned headdress

ROLLS, COILS, AND HORNS
These re-creations show some of the headdresses worn during the Middle Ages. Many were very elaborate.

EARLY HIPPIES?
From the 12th century, and especially in the latter half of the 14th century, women parted their hair in the center and allowed it to fall over the shoulders in braids or coils that often reached the knees. False hair was frequently used to increase the length of the hair. In this picture, taken from a 14th-century manuscript, the handmaid's hair is covered with a "guimpe," a piece of white linen or silk that was fastened to the hair above the ears.

THE STEEPLE
The "hennin", or steeple, headdresses were very fashionable in France. Most spectacular of all the headdresses was the "butterfly," which consisted of a wire structure that supported a veil in the shape of a butterfly's wings.

Low-cut front

14th-century leather shoes

Leaf design made by scraping away the surface of the leather

LONG SHOES
Reaching an amazing length of 18 in (46 cm), men's shoes grew ever more pointed and spiky; the toes were stuffed with moss to preserve their shape. Such shoes were considered by the clergy to be the work of the devil!

COLORFUL KNIGHTS
Knights of the 14th and 15th centuries were known for their brightly colored garments. A knight who represented a great family would be known by that family's colors, for example, the red or green knight. They also adorned their horses to complement their color and crests.

BUCKLES AND BROOCHES
To keep together the elaborate costumes of the day, silversmiths were much in demand. They created intricate clasps and buckles. The Saxon brooch on the left is known as a "caterpillar" brooch because of its arched shape; on the right is an 11th-century belt buckle with a design of animal heads.

HATS GALORE
Headwear became increasingly popular throughout the 15th century. In Quentin Massys's painting "The Money Changer and His Wife" we see the type of hat that was worn by both sexes. Some had flat crowns with narrow or turned-back brims, and all were made mainly of felt.

PILGRIMS' PROGRESS
In England the harsh weather forced pilgrims like these on their way to Canterbury to wear long, heavy robes and hats over their "coifs" (close-fitting caps tied under the chin).

A LADY STEPS OUT
This is a re-creation of what a mid-14th-century lady of the aristocracy might wear. The sideless "surcoat" – an overdress with cutout sides – is of deep red brocade and trimmed with fur. The lifted skirt reveals the plain "undercoat" – a slim-fitting robe with long, narrow sleeves. Sometimes the undercoat was of a richly patterned fabric, with the surcoat in plain velvet. Often the waist of the undercoat was encircled with a jeweled girdle.

Rich, flowing, and heavy!

THE RENAISSANCE (14th–17th centuries) really belonged to the Italians, who loved display, adored playacting, and wore the best and most expensive clothes they could afford. The soft, fluid elegance of Italian fashion matched the idealization of the human form, which is seen throughout Italian Renaissance art. During this period, influences were felt from all over Europe, especially from Spain. Low-cut dresses were shaped to emphasize the bust, which was either covered with transparent fabric or left bare. Gowns in heavy silks and full-flowing shapes were often richly embroidered and worn with bold jewelry.

Even when out hunting, the ladies were elegantly dressed

Doublet (close-fitting jacket)

Broken sleeve

Codpiece

IN THE CORNFIELDS
In stark contrast to the sumptuous costumes of the aristocracy, these Flemish peasants are dressed in the practical clothes worn by working people.

ITALIAN STYLE
This theater costume shows what a fashionable young Renaissance man would wear. A doublet of black-silk velvet is heavily overstitched in gold thread; the white shirt is threaded with a string and drawn tight at the neck – a forerunner of the ruff (pp. 20–21), which was to flourish a little later. At the elbow, the shirt shows through between the halves of the "broken" sleeve. A decorated codpiece (which sometimes doubled as a purse) is worn over a flap opening in the close-fitting hose (tights).

Hose

FLOWING FUR
Along with the fashionable short doublet and hose, a long and voluminous outer garment called a houppelande was worn. This was sometimes belted and lined in a contrasting fabric or fur.

HEAVY DRESSING
This re-creation of a late 15th-century dress is in the Italian style. The curious practice of "slashing" – slitting material and pulling the lining through – was becoming very popular (pp. 20–21). Here, the slashed sleeves reveal puffs of an undersmock.

GLOWING TAPESTRY
Both men's and women's garments were often made from richly decorated silks, damasks, and brocades, and sometimes interwoven with real gold or silver thread. Red was a particularly popular color among the upper classes – one of the demands during the Peasants' Revolt in Germany was to be allowed to wear red.

Patterned velvet

Thimbles

Needles

STITCH AND CUT
The objects shown here date from the 15th century. On the left is a fragment of hose, and above are two brass thimbles and two sewing needles. The small iron shears were used for all cutting purposes and were more common than scissors.

Hose   Shears

EARLY PLATFORMS
"Chopines" were worn over the shoes in wet weather. Some extreme versions made in Venice reached the absurd height of 30 in (76 cm) and were reputedly worn by Venetian prostitutes. This, of course, made walking without assistance some-what perilous!

Bits and pieces

ALL KINDS OF OBJECTS have been used by men and women through the ages to embellish their basic costume. Shells, beads, teeth, and feathers were all early forms of accessories, and the practice of completing a look with "extra" items continues today. As each new fashion has appeared, new or restyled accessories have followed. Often these have indicated their owner's status; handkerchiefs edged with lace, diamond-studded buckles on shoes, and wigs made from human hair were once the accessories of the wealthy. These extras have sometimes become symbols of a period – such as the large ruffs of the 16th century (pp. 20–21), or the long cigarette holders of the 1920s.

TAKING SNUFF
Snuff, or powdered tobacco, became fashionable in the 1670s and was used by both men and women until the early 19th century. One of the two early 18th-century snuffboxes shown here bears a portrait of Charles I of England.

CLOAK FASTENER
Ornaments and jewelry were worn extensively by the Romans (pp. 10–11). This is part of a chain that was used for fastening cloaks. It dates from the Roman occupation of Britain.

DETACHABLE CUFFS
During the 18th century, separate cuffs were tacked onto elbow-length sleeves so that they could be detached for cleaning or for wearing with another dress (pp. 30–31). They were usually made of fine lace or embroidered muslin, like this pair.

VIKING BROOCH
The Vikings were also fond of metal ornaments such as rings, necklets, armlets, buckles, and brooches (pp. 12–13). This brooch would have been used to fasten clothes together.

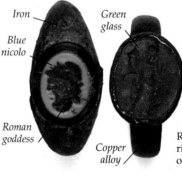

Iron

Blue nicolo

Green glass

Roman goddess

Copper alloy

RINGS AND THINGS
The Romans loved their jewelry: necklaces, bracelets, rings, armlets, and anklets were all worn frequently. Gold rings were particularly popular for both men and women (pp.10–11). It was the Romans who first used gold rings as a sign of betrothal, or marriage.

GREEK GEM
This fine gold necklace is Greek, and dates from around the third century B.C. The lions' eyes are filled with bluish-green enamel.

HAIRPINS
The elaborate hairstyles of Roman women (pp. 10–11) required hairpins like these made of jet, copper alloy, and bone. They kept the hair in place.

PATCHBOXES
The fashion for patches, or "beauty spots," was at its height in the 18th century (pp. 32–33), although it continued into the early decades of the 19th century. Patches were carried around in boxes made of wood, cardboard, china, or metal. These boxes were often decorated with miniature scenes.

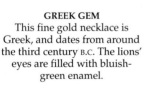

FUNCTIONAL FANS
Fans have been used since very early times as a decorative item for creating a cool current of air around the head. This 17th-century engraving depicts an Italian noblewoman flourishing her fan.

This selection of mittens dates from around 1835

FINE MITTENS
Although a form of mitten was worn for centuries as a "working" hand cover, mittens became a fashionable accessory in their own right in the 18th and through the 19th centuries. Mittens were made from embroidered net or lace, and were either crocheted or knitted. Ladies of this period wore their mittens indoors, and they could be either wrist-length (pp. 40–41) or elbow-length.

The folding feather fan, like this ostrich-feather one, was popular from the 19th century until the 1920s.

This group of 19th-century trinkets is made up of a gold filigree posy, or flower, holder (top left), a cameo brooch (above), and a gold-embossed English sovereign case.

GAUNTLET GLOVES
Both men and women of the 17th century favored the gauntlet glove (pp. 26–27). These men's gloves from that period have raised embroidery and fringe trimming on the gauntlet.

Gauntlet

PAINTED FAN
This style of folding fan originated in the Far East. This particular 18th-century fan is printed with music.

LITTLE STOCKINGS
Like their other clothes, 18th-century children's stockings were like those of their parents (pp. 32–33). This child's stocking is made of silk; it was probably worn for "good." The child would have worn similar stockings made of cotton around the home.

PRETTY PARASOL
Umbrellas and parasols were first carried in France in the 18th century. From then on, the parasol became an important fashion accessory, right through the 19th century. This delicate lace parasol dates from the 1880s.

NIMBLE FINGERS
This sewing kit covered most needs of the 19th-century woman it belonged to. As well as scissors, needles, thimble, and bodkin (blunt, large-eyed needle), it contains buttonhooks for fastening boots and gloves.

Slashes galore

EUROPE WAS ON the brink of a new era in 1500: universities were booming, books were being printed, the Americas had been discovered – the world was becoming Europeanized. Early in the century, men's fashions continued to be influenced by Italy, France, and Belgium. By the second decade, it was Germany that took the lead in fashion; clothes were brightly colored and the German custom of "slashing"– cutting into fabric to allow the material underneath to show through – was widespread. Fashion changed dramatically in the middle of the century when the Spanish look arrived. Stripes were a feature, as well as capes, which could be either short or long. With the emergence of the new middle class, the bourgeois businessman and his wife were able to wear less expensive versions of upper-class fashions, although they remained about 10 years out of date.

The look of the day: slashed doublet and short cape

Whalebone or metal strips at sides maintained shape of belly

SHOEHORN *right*
This original shoehorn is from around 1590 and is engraved with the figure of a man in contemporary costume. Many articles such as this were finely hand-etched with figures, animals, or flowing heraldic designs.

PEASANT GEAR
This engraving by Albrecht Dürer (1471–1528) shows three German peasants wearing short-belted doublets. The man on the right is wearing high riding boots and spurs.

PUNCHED JERKIN
This is an original Spanish-style leather jerkin from the late 16th century. The high neck supported a ruff, and the leather is covered in broad stripes created by a punched design.

PAUNCHY PUNCH
The Punch figure on the far left is showing off the pease-cod belly, or goose-belly, which originated in Spain. Men padded the fronts of their doublets to form an artificial paunch shape. The false bellies were created by tailors with horsehair (left), rags, or sometimes wool.

Horsehair

These shoes are nearly 500 years old!

STEPPING OUT
Early in the 16th century, shoes became so wide that in England Henry VIII issued an order limiting their width to a maximum of 6 in (15 cm). Square-ended shoes often were low-cut and fastened with a strap across the instep. Heels did not appear until the end of the century.

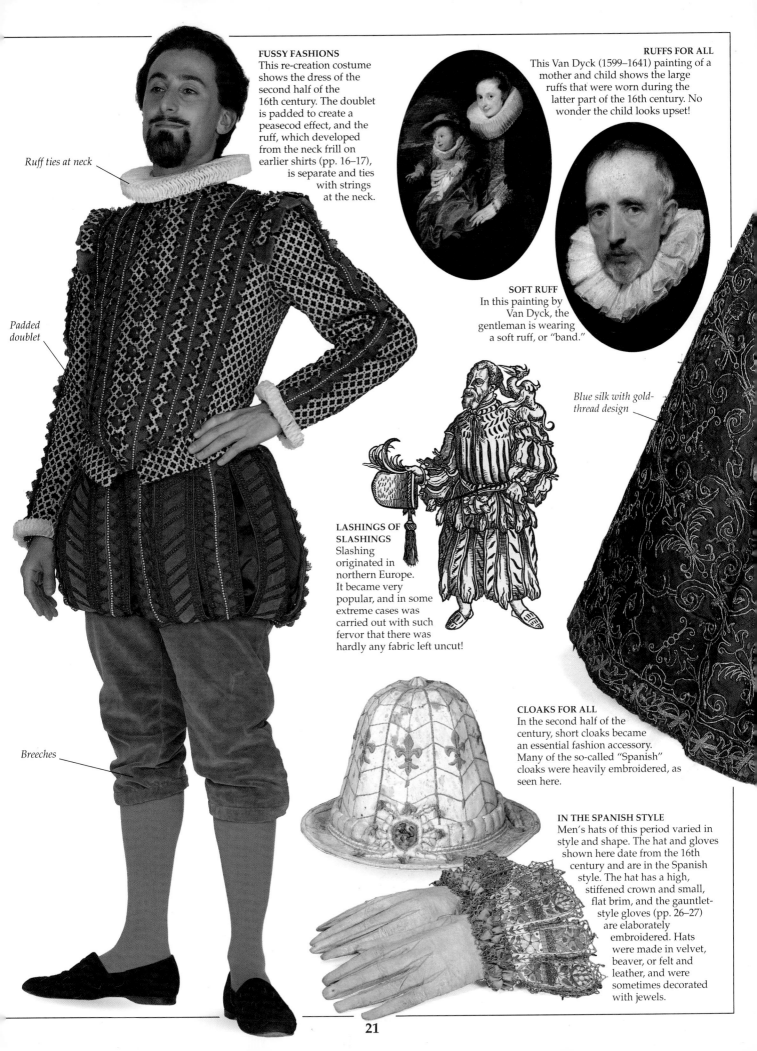

FUSSY FASHIONS
This re-creation costume shows the dress of the second half of the 16th century. The doublet is padded to create a peasecod effect, and the ruff, which developed from the neck frill on earlier shirts (pp. 16–17), is separate and ties with strings at the neck.

Ruff ties at neck

Padded doublet

Breeches

RUFFS FOR ALL
This Van Dyck (1599–1641) painting of a mother and child shows the large ruffs that were worn during the latter part of the 16th century. No wonder the child looks upset!

SOFT RUFF
In this painting by Van Dyck, the gentleman is wearing a soft ruff, or "band."

Blue silk with gold-thread design

LASHINGS OF SLASHINGS
Slashing originated in northern Europe. It became very popular, and in some extreme cases was carried out with such fervor that there was hardly any fabric left uncut!

CLOAKS FOR ALL
In the second half of the century, short cloaks became an essential fashion accessory. Many of the so-called "Spanish" cloaks were heavily embroidered, as seen here.

IN THE SPANISH STYLE
Men's hats of this period varied in style and shape. The hat and gloves shown here date from the 16th century and are in the Spanish style. The hat has a high, stiffened crown and small, flat brim, and the gauntlet-style gloves (pp. 26–27) are elaborately embroidered. Hats were made in velvet, beaver, or felt and leather, and were sometimes decorated with jewels.

Bells and boxes

ToWARD THE MIDDLE of the 16th century, Spanish fashions dominated Europe. Out went bright colors and easy flowing lines, and in came the rigid extravagance and somber colors of the Spanish court. Although this was one of the most ostentatious periods in fashion, it was also one of the most uncomfortable: for men, the belly was padded to create a potbellied effect (pp. 20–21), and the trunk hose (full knickerbockers) were stuffed with horsehair and wool. In 1555, the ruff emerged, sometimes extending as much as 9 in (23 cm) from the neck. Women wore boned bodices, rigid "stomachers," to keep the bodice (upper part of dress) firm and smooth, and farthingales – a series of hoops worn under skirts.

Fan ruff

Until the middle of the century, northern fashions dominated. This engraving by Dutch artist Hans Holbein shows a woman in typical northern dress.

Stomacher

Children's clothes were simply copies of adult fashions in the 16th century

BOHEMIAN STYLE
In this detail from an early 17th-century painting of Elizabeth of Bohemia by Robert Peake the Elder, we can see how the striped silk dress has been designed to emphasize the shape created by the "wheel" farthingale (right). Elizabeth is also wearing a "stomacher" – a decorative, V-shaped panel worn attached to, or separate from, the dress – and an open, or fan, ruff, worn by unmarried women at ceremonial occasions. Shoes were visible for the first time.

CASKET OF GOLD
This small leather jewel casket dates from the 16th century and is typical of the caskets used by families to store their valuables at home. The casket contains four gold rings of the period.

TAILOR-MADE
This northern Italian tailor is wearing a typical middle-class outfit from the second half of the 16th century. His trunk hose (knickerbockers) would have been padded with horsehair or wool.

Jacket is decorated with quilted stitch

This detail is from a portrait by Giovanni Moroni, c. 1571

HANDMADE
The elaborate garments of the 16th century were made by tradesmen working alone or in small groups. Incredibly, all sewing was done by hand.

NATURAL COLORS
The sumptuous colored fabrics used to create the dresses of the early 16th century were achieved with natural dyes – from plants and their roots. Material was dyed in large vats and hung to dry on wooden poles.

This style of headdress was worn only in Germany

BOX DRESS
This English-style dress shows the extent to which the "look" of the period dominated women's fashion. The farthingale reached its widest form (as wide as the shoulders), creating a boxlike effect.

The "wheel" farthingale, worn under the dress above and on the left

BELL-SHAPED
Farthingales originated in Spain in the mid-16th century. They consisted of simple underskirts supported by graduated hoops of whalebone, wire, or cane, which produced a bell-shaped silhouette.

GERMAN STYLE
This German gentleman is wearing a gown resembling the houppelande (pp. 16–17) over his doublet and breeches. His wife wears a balloon headdress.

Fancy feet

Boots, sandals, and shoes originally evolved from the basic need to protect the feet, but as with hats (pp. 46–47), footwear became an important accessory in its own right. Shoes have come in many different styles over the ages – from those of the 15th century with long, pointed toes (pp. 14–15), to the plain, square-toed shoes of the 16th century (pp. 20–21), to the fine, lavishly decorated shoes of the 18th century (pp. 30–33), and on to the chunky, high platform shoes of the 1970s (bottom right). Although most shoes are made of leather or suede, other materials have included rubber, canvas, silk, satin, and brocade.

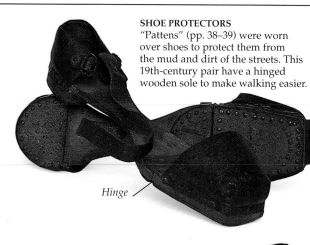

SHOE PROTECTORS
"Pattens" (pp. 38–39) were worn over shoes to protect them from the mud and dirt of the streets. This 19th-century pair have a hinged wooden sole to make walking easier.

Hinge

PRESERVED IN MUD
This man's leather shoe was found at the bottom of a river and is thought to date back to the 1660s.

This boot is more than 500 years old – it dates from c. 1430

POINTED SHOES
"Poulaines," or pointed shoes, like this date from the 15th century (pp. 14–15). They either curled up at the toe or were flat.

A VERY OLD BOOT
This short leather boot belonged to a mid-15th-century man. Soon after this, shoes became shorter and rounder (pp. 20–21).

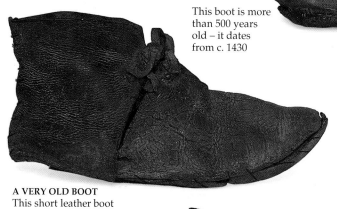

SILK ANKLE BOOT
Women's silk ankle boots like these that laced up at the side were fashionable around the mid-19th century.

CYCLING BOOTS?
These kid knee-length boots may well have been worn with a cycling bloomer outfit in the early 20th century.

Snakeskin

SKIN SHOES
Reptile-skin shoes, handbags, and belts were popular in the late 1920s. This led to the killing of many crocodiles, alligators, and snakes to cater to the fashion whims of the time.

CREAM SUEDE SHOES
These smart suede women's shoes are typical of the luxurious 1920s style.

Ribbon rosettes

Ruched silk

FOR INDOORS ONLY
When entertaining at home, a fashionable 19th-century lady would probably have worn leather mules like these with a loose-fitting "tea" gown.

These mules date from the 1870s

Pleated silk edging

PRETTY PUMPS
Leather pumps like these would have been worn at home only. This pair dates from 1860.

STEEL BEADS
Shoes like these were very fashionable in the early 20th century, but would not look out of place today. They are decorated with fine steel beads.

DELICATE BOOTS
These satin boots from the 1880s fasten with tabs and buttons at the front.

Silk has started to split with age

Strap-and-buckle fastening

WALKING SHOES
These black leather walking shoes date from around 1914.

WHICH ONES?
Shoes have long been an important fashion accessory as well as a means of protecting the feet. Choosing the right shoes can take a long time!

Men's lace-up platforms from the early 1970s

SIGNS OF AGE
The silk of this woman's shoe is beginning to rot and split. Considering the shoe is about 300 years old, it has aged pretty well!

PLATFORMS
Both men and women wore platform shoes in the 1970s. Some platform shoes, especially those with wooden soles, were rather heavy and difficult to walk in.

Ribbons and bows

French fashions excelled in loops, bows, and flounces

THE FASHION PENDULUM of the 17th century swung between the extremes of puritan sobriety in England and Holland and excessive flamboyance at the French court. Early in the century, the stiff Spanish fashions that had prevailed (pp. 22–23) gave way to a more natural look. As France became a great power under Louis XIV's leadership, French style dominated European fashion. From the 1660s, the French court dictated an exuberant display of ribbons, curls, flounces, and feathers – the men often more frivolous and extreme in their dress than the women. Although French fashion came to a standstill between 1674 and 1678 when a royal edict forbade luxury, this was soon forgotton and the streets were once again filled with new designs and styles.

Ribbons on hat

Falling ruff

Ribbons around the waist

Ribbons on the "skirt"

DASHING CAVALIERS
The streets of England, France, and Holland were filled with cavaliers, or mounted soldiers. This etching of the famous Three Musketeers from the book by Alexandre Dumas shows the fashion of the time: short coats, decorated breeches, bucket-topped boots, long hair, lace-edged collars, and wide-brimmed hats with feathers.

FEATHER CURLER
This 17th-century bone feather curler was discovered in London. The feathers that were so fashionable for hats and fans were dyed in the current colors and then curled.

Ribbon bows on shoes

Square-toed shoes

THE TRIANGULAR MAN
This figure, taken from a painting by the Dutch artist Ter Borch (1617–1681), is wearing the voluminous petticoat breeches that came into fashion around the middle of the 17th century. They were so wide that they became skirts, and were usually trimmed with rows of ribbon loops at the hem and waist. The shirt, which became looser and softer, was exposed at the waist and sleeves by the short jerkin. The stiff, upright ruff of earlier times became the falling ruff.

DRAMATIC SIMPLICITY

In the 1640s and 1650s, the Puritans in England rejected flamboyant fashions and turned to the austerity of the Protestant and Nonconformist churches. The typical outfit – "sugarloaf" hat, plain white collar, hooded cape – was also worn by the Dutch middle classes. The Pilgrims took this style with them to America, where it was adopted for nearly a century.

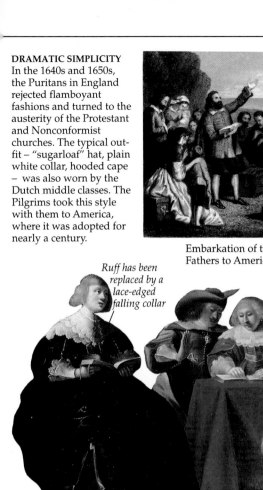

Embarkation of the Pilgrim Fathers to America

Ruff has been replaced by a lace-edged falling collar

Embroidered bird motif on gauntlet

GAUNTLET GLOVES

Gloves, already an important fashion accessory in the 16th century (pp. 20–21), became even more noticeable in the 17th century. Generally, they were imported from Spain and made of soft leather with deep, flaring gauntlets covered in intricate embroidery (pp. 18–19). The white leather gloves shown here are from 1670.

"ELEGANT FIGURES"

This detail from "An Interior with Elegant Figures Reading," by Anthoine Palamedesz, shows clearly how the stiff upright fashions of the 16th century changed to a softer look.

Baldric buckle

Breeches buckle

Breeches buckle

Baldric buckle

BUCKLE UP

Along with bows, ribbons, and straps, buckles were seen everywhere in the 17th century. A multitude of materials were worked into decorative shapes for belts, straps, baldrics (pp. 28–29), and breeches. Around 1670, the buckle replaced the bow on the instep of shoes.

FOLDING FANS

Folding fans arrived in Europe in the 16th century from China, where they had been used for more than 500 years. This late 17th-century fan has been preserved in its original case.

NOT QUITE TRAINERS

This child's leather shoe from early in the 17th century has a tongue and ties known as "latches." The shoes could be worn on either foot.

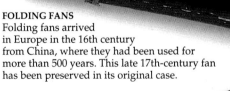

HIGH HEELS ARRIVE

High heels became established in the 17th century. Toward the end of the century heels were often several inches high, and toes were very long and squared off.

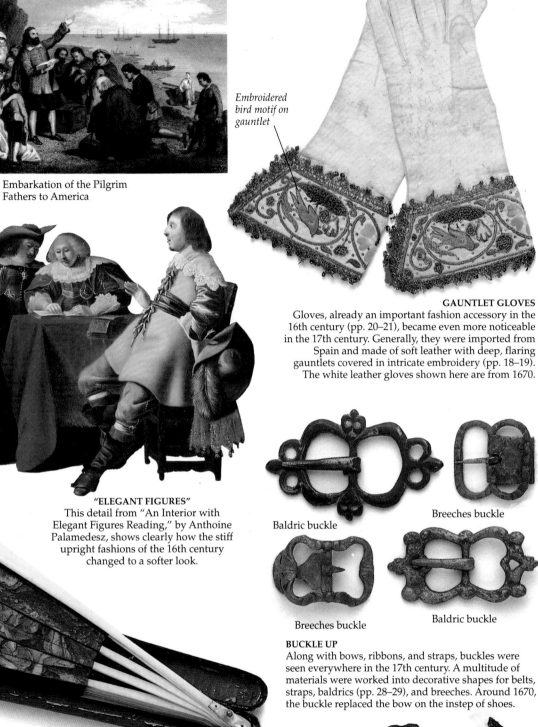

A flourish of curls

Spectacles were invented as early as 1300. Because most people could not read, spectacles were considered proof of an educated person. Side-pieces did not appear until the 18th century.

THE FASHION WORLD, along with many other aspects of French life, was dominated by the French king Louis XIV (1638–1715). It was Louis who introduced the periwig – later known simply as a wig – to the French court, some say in order to hide his own baldness. Soon the "full-bottomed" periwig symbolized authority and dignity, and no civilized gentleman was seen without one. Heads were either shaved, or the hair cut very short. Working men did not wear wigs, as they were expensive and cumbersome, but they grew their own hair long instead. Although women's hairstyles did not attain the splendor of men's wigs, the "fontanges" appeared in the 1690s – a complex scaffolding of muslin, lace, and ribbons, all mounted on a wire frame. These tall, fluted concoctions towered up to 8 in (20 cm) above the head, but gradually shrank in size to fit into the small, round caps of the 18th century.

MOURNING TIME
When somebody died, the close family of the deceased was expected to go into mourning for about a year, which meant wearing black clothes and special jewelry such as this. Finger rings fashioned as skeletons, coffins, and skulls were distributed to relatives at funerals.

Skeleton

Skeleton pendant

Mourning rings

Pearls surround glass stone

GERMAN GENTS
These two German men show the prevailing style of around 1670. Both are wearing the shallow crown hat with the broad, curving brim that was to develop into the "tricorn" (three-cornered hat). Square-toed shoes were popular – the tops were sometimes turned down to show the lining.

BUTTON BOX
Buttons were used on everything in the 17th century – wide, full cuffs, jackets, vests, sleeves, and shoes. Many of them were quite elaborate, as this set of buttons and studs dated 1680 shows.

Buttons are set with "paste" – used for making imitation gems

Stud

Iron compartment opens here

FLATIRON
With so much white linen showing at cuff and neck, constant ironing was essential. This flatiron from the late 17th century was used by putting a heated stone in a compartment in its base.

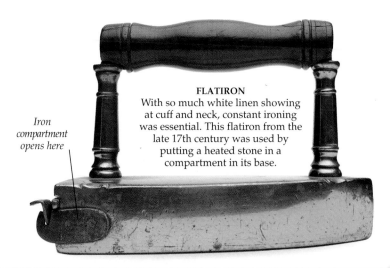

Two-horned wig

WONDROUS WIGS
Periwigs were quite elaborate by 1680. The full-bottomed wig for men, although very large and heavy, was considered essential (left). More extreme versions rose on top of the head in two horns (full figure), while some men preferred their own hair and wore a wig of curled bangs to add height (right).

Cravat

Ivory comb of 1660

Bone comb

Deep, buttoned-back cuffs

COMBS IN BONE
In the late 17th century, women curled and dressed their own hair. Combs were hand-cut in various materials, including bone and ivory.

OUT FOR A STROLL
The well-dressed gentleman often wore a "baldric" – a belt or sash worn over the shoulder and across the body to carry a sword or a walking stick. This walking stick dates from the late 17th century.

Ivory head worked in scroll design

Full-skirted jacket

Children wore smaller versions of adult clothes

THE BIRTH OF THE "SUIT"
This theatrical costume depicts the late 17th-century gentleman. It was in this century that men's clothing gradually evolved into what we now call a suit. The long jacket, based on the cassock, a long, close-fitting garment worn by the clergy, was originally worn buttoned but was increasingly left undone. By the 1690s, the coat or jacket was full-skirted with two groups of fan pleats at the back. The deep cuffs buttoned back, and the bib of the earlier part of the century had been replaced by the cravat, a scarf worn around the neck. Costume at this time varied somewhat according to the wearer's religious and political beliefs.

DOING THE DISHES
For everyday chores, women often folded back their skirts or wrapped material around their waists to protect their dresses. The peasant classes wore simple styles that copied details such as collars from the upper classes.

Silk and brocade

THERE WERE SEVERAL STYLES OF DRESS for women during the 18th century. The first was the "mantua," a gown that was fitted into the waist at the back and worn open at the front to show a matching or contrasting petticoat that was sometimes quilted for extra warmth and bulk. From this evolved the graceful "sac," or sack dress, with pleats at the back that hung unfitted from the shoulders. A further development of this dress was the "polonaise" style, with its overskirt draped up at three points to show a decorative underskirt – a particular favorite of the French queen Marie Antoinette.

STREET FASHION
This scene illustrates a life-style far removed from the splendor shown on these pages. Ordinary people wore simple clothes, often hand-me-downs or homemade garments of wool or cotton.

SACKBACK
This original silk brocade dress of the 1770s shows clearly the pleated back that gave this style its name. The fitted bodice, which had by now replaced the stomacher (p. 22) was fastened at the front and laced up at the back under the pleat. The open-fronted skirt revealed a matching petticoat.

Back view of dress

Silk floral brocade

Detachable lace cuffs could be removed for cleaning

18th-century side panniers with cane stiffeners

FALSE HIPS
Dresses like the one on the left were supported at the hip by a "pannier," introduced in France in about 1718. These varied in size and shape – some royal court dresses were extremely wide and required a more robust pannier!

Opening for hand

HIDDEN POCKETS
Pockets were not sewn into garments until the 19th century. Eighteenth-century pockets were made in pairs and attached to a tape that was tied around the waist under the skirt. They were reached through a slit in the skirt.

OUT OF THE MUD
This 1740 green brocade shoe has been preserved with its "clog". The clog was worn under the shoe out of doors to protect it from the mud and dirt of the streets.

Hook for hanging over belt

Lady's leather purse

Gentleman's leather pouch bag

BAGS AND PURSES
Handbags became an indispensable fashion accessory in the late 18th and early 19th centuries. Ladies and gentlemen carried their possessions in bags like these. Men sometimes hung money pouches on their belts.

Lady's satin bag

FRENCH TRENDSETTERS
Many fashion trends of this period were set in France. It was said that when the latest French fashion became popular in England it was already becoming outdated in Paris.

This fichu dates from 1735

Silk gauze with hand-embroidered flowers

THIN SHAWL
Most ladies wore a small scarf called a "fichu." It was draped around the shoulders and tucked into a low neckline. Later fichus were longer and made of muslin or lawn (fine cotton or linen). These were crossed over the bust and knotted at the back.

GENTLEMEN'S STOCKINGS
This gentleman's stocking dates from the middle of the 18th century, by which time stockings had lost their bright colors (pp. 32–33). By 1780, they were usually made of wool.

Stockings were held up by ribbons tied above the knee

The long, full wigs of the previous century (pp. 28–29) were replaced in the 1720s by tie wigs

Deep, turned-back cuffs allowed lace sleeve to fall onto the hand

Long vest

VELVET SUIT
This is a reproduction of an early 18th-century suit. The velvet coat is typical of that worn by a young professional gentleman of the time. It has rows of buttons at the front, which were usually left undone. The vest was long, and the breeches were loose and comfortable, with a simple fly opening. As vests became shorter and breeches more visible, breeches were cut more closely over the thigh and knees (pp. 32–33).

Powder and patches

W EALTHY MEN AND WOMEN of the 18th century wore tall, white powdered wigs, first introduced in about 1710. Working men did not wear wigs, as they were both expensive and cumbersome. Very white skin was also considered attractive for both men and women; the addition of rouge brought color to the lips and cheeks. It was also stylish to wear black beauty patches. These were cut to various designs, including sun, moon, and star shapes. As washing was considered unhealthy, the heavy makeup and beauty patches of this period helped cover the layers of dirt and skin blemishes caused by disease. Perfume was also used by both sexes in an attempt to disguise any unfortunate odors!

The powder used to whiten wigs was usually white starch or rice flour

Cravat

Slim sleeves

Coat has lost back pleats

MACARONI MEN
This reproduction costume shows how menswear developed during the 18th century. The coat is narrower than the earlier version (pp. 30–31) and has lost the heavy back pleats. Both sleeves and breeches are slimmer, and the vest is shorter. A group of Englishmen known as "Macaronis" exaggerated this style by adding decorations such as enormous shoe buckles and very large buttons.

BRILLIANT BUCKLES
Until about 1720, shoe buckles were usually of small rectangular or oval shapes. As these three original later buckles show, they gradually became larger and more extravagant. Rich people attending court wore diamond and silver buckles, while the less wealthy wore buckles made of steel, brass, pinchbeck (copper and zinc alloy), and quartz.

HOOPED SKIRT
France set the fashion for this 18th-century dress with its dome-shaped hooped skirt. The look is completed by a large hat perched at an odd angle.

Mount is made of chicken skin – a name given to thin kidskin

SKIN FAN
It was during the 18th century that fans were at their most elaborate. Artists were commissioned to paint scenes on the silk or skin "mounts," and the fans were sometimes encrusted with jewels.

Carved ivory sticks

Gentleman's silk stocking

SILKY LEGS
The 17th-century fashion for bright stocking colors continued into the early part of the 18th century. The best quality stockings were made of silk, and many were highly decorated.

HORSE OR HUMAN?
The finest wigs of this period were made of human hair. However, as these were expensive, horsehair became a popular cheaper alternative. It also had another advantage – it did not uncurl in the rain!

LITTLE ADULTS
This painting by William Hogarth, dated 1742, illustrates what little difference there was between children's and adult's clothes.

Folding 18th-century comb

Wooden wig curlers

Silk wig bag

WIG BAG
Often the tail of the wig, which hung down at the back, was encased in a black silk bag drawn up with cords at the nape, or back of the neck, and finished with a black bow.

HOT HAIR
Women's hairstyles and wigs were so high and voluminous during the 1770s and 1780s that they ran the risk of being set on fire by chandelier candles!

COURT COAT
European royal courts have always been noted for their splendor, and those of the 18th century were no exception. This original gentleman's court coat is beautifully embroidered with lilies of the valley and other small flowers.

Pocket opening

INTRICATE STITCHES
This detail from another original dark-blue silk court coat shows clearly the fine embroidery typical of the 18th century.

DRESS VESTS
These original vests are also good examples of the quality needlework of this period. Although professional embroiderers existed, much of the work was done by women at home. Once embroidered, the panels would be sent to a tailor, who would make them into vests.

Bathing beauties

PUBLIC BATHING was very popular around 350 B.C. in Greece and ancient Rome, where men and women wore togas as opposed to special bathing clothes. After this period, water pursuits were not revived until the 18th century, when the medicinal properties of spa and sea waters were greatly advocated. Men bathed naked, while women changed into a flannel shift with long sleeves within the private confines of a horse-drawn hut on wheels that carried them into the sea! It was not until bathing became a public activity in the early 19th century that swimwear design became important.

Sunglasses were introduced in 1885 but did not become fashionable until the 1930s

INTO THE BOUNDING WAVES!
From the turn of the 20th century, women's swimwear gradually became briefer and more functional, as this 1902 cotton outfit shows.

BATHING BLOOMERS
Corseted, bloomer-style costumes made from serge, a strong, twilled fabric, and trimmed with braid were standard wear for women and girls in France and England by the 1860s.

SECOND SKIN
These 1920s tubular wool costumes clung to the body and were thought very revealing at the time. The bold geometric designs reflect the fashion of the middle of the decade.

Harlequin design

THIRTIES TARTAN
Throughout the 1930s, the knitted one-piece was dominant, with the waist and bust a little more defined than in the 1920s. Some had halter necks, like this tartan wool costume. The man is also wearing a fashionable one-piece costume, which has a "modesty" skirt like that of the woman's. It was not until the mid-1930s that men began to wear trunks and that the two-piece was introduced for women.

BONES AND FRILLS
The bust of this 1950s costume is boned. The back is ruched, or gathered, with elastic, and the short skirt has rows of frills.

SILKY SUIT
This 1920s swimsuit is made from a silky black jersey. The extra fabric sewn into the skirt gives fullness at the hips.

DRY HAIR
Bathing hats of all materials and styles kept the hair dry and out of the eyes. This elasticized rubber hat dates from around 1915.

Buttons allow for easy putting on and taking off

DARK IS SAFE
Most swimsuits were made in dark colors at this time because pale ones became transparent when wet! This man's bathing costume, made of cotton stockingette, dates from 1909.

BRIEF BRIEFS
This 1970s style of bikini is known as a "string" bikini because it has string ties for the halter bra and tiny pants.

Mob cap

PRETTY DEMURE
From the late 19th century, the legs and arms of women's swimwear shortened. This 1890s costume has knee-length drawers under a tunic.

Optional halter strap

PLAYSUIT
This floral-printed sunsuit dates from the 1940s. It buttons down the bodice, or upper part, along the waist, and down the side.

NOT ITSY-BITSY, TEENY-WEENY
The bikini first arrived in 1946. This boldly printed 1950s bikini has waist-high pants and both halter and shoulder straps.

HOT AND HEAVY
Hand-knitted swimsuits like this one from the 1930s were hot to wear and stretched and became particularly heavy when wet.

This and that

This container for smelling salts dates from the 19th century

THROUGHOUT TIME, fashion has dictated various basic elements of style, such as the height of the waist, the length of the skirt, the length and shape of the sleeve, and the height of the heel. But it is possibly the fads and crazes for the "extras" to go with the outfit that really define an age and add life to what we wear. In days gone by it was snuffboxes, walking sticks, and silk garters; in the 20th century, a new material – plastic – changed the meaning of the word "accessory." Soon, fantastic shapes, sizes, and colors of plastic jewelry, handbags, and belts were spilling out of shops. Sunglasses, which arrived in the 1930s, have remained a "must" for every would-be socialite and movie star.

Ring for looping holder around the little finger

RING-AROUND-THE-POSY
Small posies of sweet-smelling flowers were carried in decorative holders by 19th-century ladies to disguise the not-so-pleasant sewage smells around them! The posy-holders were often as intricate as pieces of jewelry.

Wedding posy-holder from 1861

Posy-holders could also be pinned to clothes

Pince-nez, c. 1930s

Tortoiseshell lorgnettes, c. 1880s

Gold lorgnettes, late 19th century

Gilt spyglass, c. 1800

WHAT A SPECTACLE!
Eyeglasses and spectacles were used from around the late 13th century (pp. 28–29). Some, like the "pince-nez," just balanced or were held on the nose, while others were held in the hand – the "spyglass" – or could be folded up, like the "lorgnette."

Cap is decorated with appliquéd animals

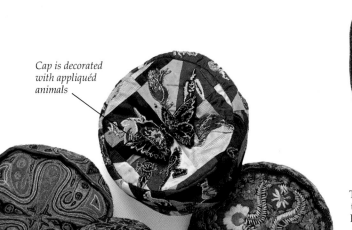

EGYPTIAN INFLUENCE
The discovery of Tutankhamen's tomb in 1922 inspired a wave of Egyptian themes in fashion. The colors of this beaded handbag, which is decorated with a winged sphinx, are typically Egyptian.

Homemade silk tango knickers, c. 1914

PIPES AND CAPS
This selection of 19th-century "smoking caps" is typical of those that men wore at home when relaxing or smoking (pp. 46–47). The caps were usually highly embroidered, and many had tassels. Smoking caps were often the handiwork of wives and daughters.

Pipe, c. 1880

Pipe bowl is carved in the shape of a woman's head

LET'S DANCE!
The tango originated in South America during the 1920s and quickly spread to Europe. The energetic and exciting rhythms required unrestrictive clothing. Some enthusiasts made their own tango knickers – made from one length of material with two openings for the legs.

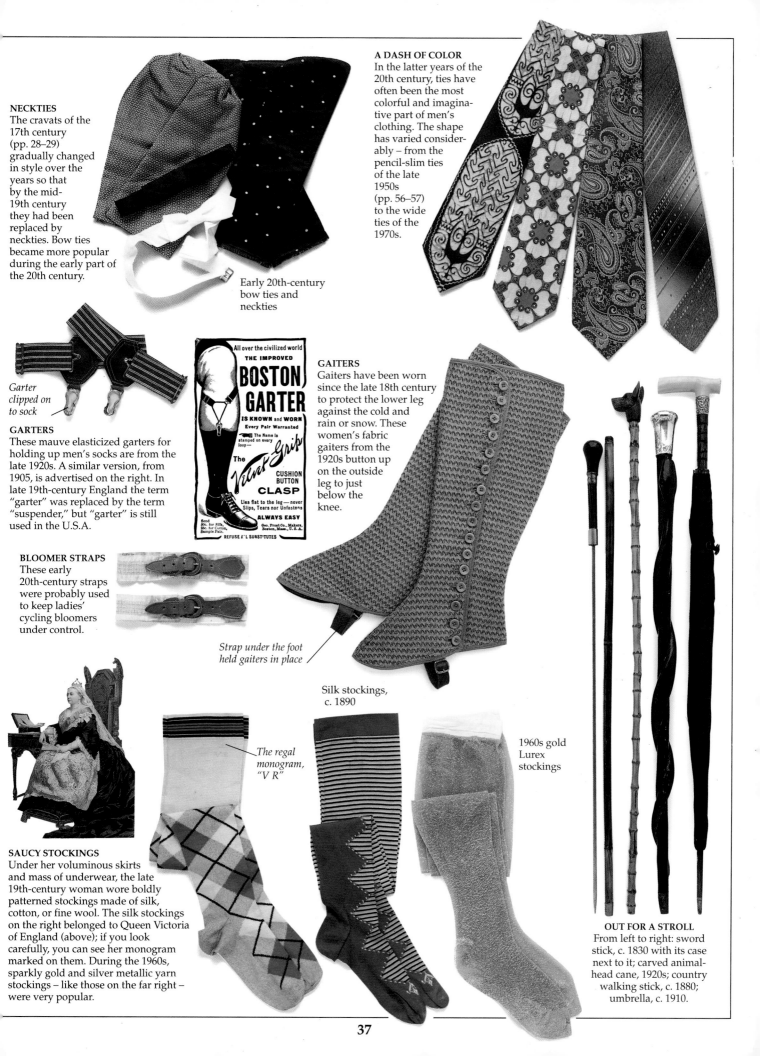

NECKTIES
The cravats of the 17th century (pp. 28–29) gradually changed in style over the years so that by the mid-19th century they had been replaced by neckties. Bow ties became more popular during the early part of the 20th century.

Early 20th-century bow ties and neckties

A DASH OF COLOR
In the latter years of the 20th century, ties have often been the most colorful and imaginative part of men's clothing. The shape has varied considerably – from the pencil-slim ties of the late 1950s (pp. 56–57) to the wide ties of the 1970s.

Garter clipped on to sock

GARTERS
These mauve elasticized garters for holding up men's socks are from the late 1920s. A similar version, from 1905, is advertised on the right. In late 19th-century England the term "garter" was replaced by the term "suspender," but "garter" is still used in the U.S.A.

All over the civilized world
THE IMPROVED
BOSTON GARTER
IS KNOWN and WORN
Every Pair Warranted
The Name is stamped on every loop—
The *Velvet Grip*
CUSHION BUTTON CLASP
Lies flat to the leg — never Slips, Tears nor Unfastens
ALWAYS EASY
Send
50c. for Silk,
25c. for Cotton,
Sample Pair.
Geo. Frost Co.. Makers,
Boston, Mass., U. S. A.
REFUSE ALL SUBSTITUTES

GAITERS
Gaiters have been worn since the late 18th century to protect the lower leg against the cold and rain or snow. These women's fabric gaiters from the 1920s button up on the outside leg to just below the knee.

BLOOMER STRAPS
These early 20th-century straps were probably used to keep ladies' cycling bloomers under control.

Strap under the foot held gaiters in place

Silk stockings, c. 1890

The regal monogram, "V R"

1960s gold Lurex stockings

SAUCY STOCKINGS
Under her voluminous skirts and mass of underwear, the late 19th-century woman wore boldly patterned stockings made of silk, cotton, or fine wool. The silk stockings on the right belonged to Queen Victoria of England (above); if you look carefully, you can see her monogram marked on them. During the 1960s, sparkly gold and silver metallic yarn stockings – like those on the far right – were very popular.

OUT FOR A STROLL
From left to right: sword stick, c. 1830 with its case next to it; carved animal-head cane, 1920s; country walking stick, c. 1880; umbrella, c. 1910.

Cotton for all

MORE COTTON
Power-loom weaving made for a greater output of cotton in the 19th century at cheaper prices than ever before.

As a result of the application of scientific and technical discoveries made in the 18th century, the textile and printing industries of the 19th century became mechanized.

New power looms and roller printing almost entirely replaced the old wooden printing blocks, resulting in a larger output of cotton material in a variety of beautiful colors and patterns at a fraction of the previous cost. At last, printed cotton fabrics were within the reach of every shopper. New power looms were able to process as much natural cotton as the U.S.A. could produce.

Detail from a painting by John Smart of the Misses Binney, dated 1806

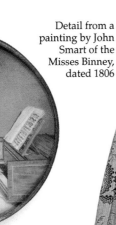

DRESSING DOWN
The influence of the French Revolution (1789–1799) spread far and wide. The brocade gowns and powdered wigs of the 18th century disappeared – to be replaced by flimsy, high-waisted dresses worn without either corset or petticoat underneath.

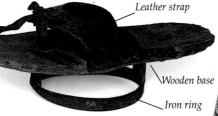

Leather strap

Wooden base

Iron ring

SHOE PROTECTORS
Overshoes, or "pattens," made of wood, leather, and metal were worn over shoes to raise them above the filthy streets. This early 19th-century patten is the sort the woman on the right would have worn.

CAPS FOR ALL
A cap was worn by most women for nearly every occasion – both indoors and out. They varied according to the woman's age and whether she was single or married.

Clasp was attached to belt

SEWING BELT
Women sometimes wore a "chatelaine" at the waist. This was a clasp with chains to which various sewing implements were attached. Made of gold, silver, or steel, chatelaines occasionally carried smelling salts and keys as well.

DRESSED IN COTTON
After the earlier flimsy dresses, the style changed to a "stiffer" look, as shown here by this original printed cotton dress of 1825. The waist is still above the natural line, but corset and petticoats were worn once again. The sleeves are long and the dress has a more modest neckline than earlier. By 1827, dresses were beginning to spread at the hem and sleeves, marking the move toward the crinoline dress that was to follow (pp. 42–43).

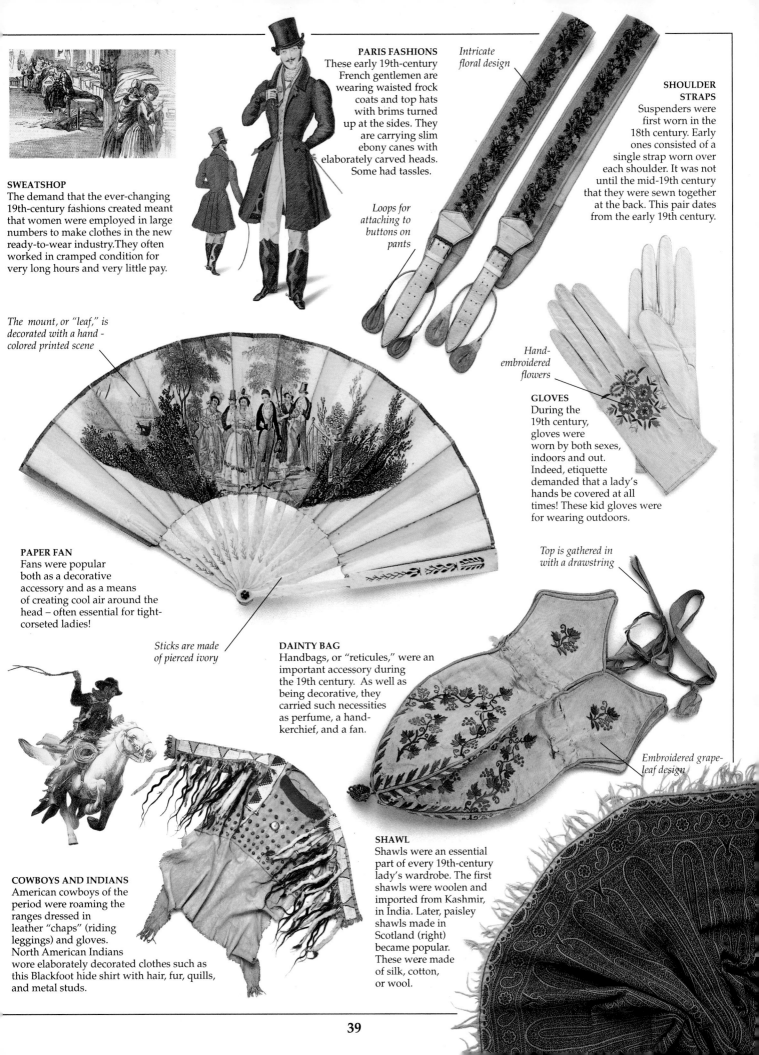

PARIS FASHIONS
These early 19th-century French gentlemen are wearing waisted frock coats and top hats with brims turned up at the sides. They are carrying slim ebony canes with elaborately carved heads. Some had tassels.

Intricate floral design

SHOULDER STRAPS
Suspenders were first worn in the 18th century. Early ones consisted of a single strap worn over each shoulder. It was not until the mid-19th century that they were sewn together at the back. This pair dates from the early 19th century.

SWEATSHOP
The demand that the ever-changing 19th-century fashions created meant that women were employed in large numbers to make clothes in the new ready-to-wear industry. They often worked in cramped condition for very long hours and very little pay.

Loops for attaching to buttons on pants

The mount, or "leaf," is decorated with a hand-colored printed scene

Hand-embroidered flowers

GLOVES
During the 19th century, gloves were worn by both sexes, indoors and out. Indeed, etiquette demanded that a lady's hands be covered at all times! These kid gloves were for wearing outdoors.

PAPER FAN
Fans were popular both as a decorative accessory and as a means of creating cool air around the head – often essential for tight-corseted ladies!

Top is gathered in with a drawstring

Sticks are made of pierced ivory

DAINTY BAG
Handbags, or "reticules," were an important accessory during the 19th century. As well as being decorative, they carried such necessities as perfume, a handkerchief, and a fan.

Embroidered grape-leaf design

COWBOYS AND INDIANS
American cowboys of the period were roaming the ranges dressed in leather "chaps" (riding leggings) and gloves. North American Indians wore elaborately decorated clothes such as this Blackfoot hide shirt with hair, fur, quills, and metal studs.

SHAWL
Shawls were an essential part of every 19th-century lady's wardrobe. The first shawls were woolen and imported from Kashmir, in India. Later, paisley shawls made in Scotland (right) became popular. These were made of silk, cotton, or wool.

The sewing machine

Two things were to have a profound effect on fashion in the second half of the 19th century – the birth of the fashion house and the invention of the sewing machine. In 1857, a young Englishman named Charles Worth set up the first "couture," or fashion, house in Paris. He had the completely new idea of preparing a collection of gowns in advance and presenting them on models to his clients. The French empress Eugénie (wife of Napoleon III) was one of his early clients, and as other ladies of the court rushed to follow her lead, his success was assured. However, the biggest impact on fashion was the introduction of the sewing machine. Although the idea of a machine to stitch cloth was first conceived by Thomas Saint, an Englishman, in 1790, the first person to produce a practical sewing machine was Isaac Merrit Singer, an American, in 1851. This machine was responsible for an entirely new concept in clothing – mass production.

EVENING FINERY
After the crinoline (pp. 42–43), the width of the skirt became concentrated at the back. This original dress from the 1880s has a plain tight bodice and skirt supported at the back by a bustle (pp. 54–55).

Silk brocade

FANCY PINS
Decorative pins like these were used to hold a gentleman's tie, cravat, or neck scarf in place. More extroverted gentlemen wore larger, more flamboyant pins.

Gold swivel-frame brooch with hairwork

CAFE SOCIETY
In the late 19th century, taking afternoon tea became a popular pastime. Teashops became places for fashionable ladies to meet and be seen in their latest outfits.

Gold and enamel "In memory of" brooch

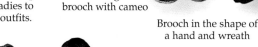

Scrolled gold brooch with cameo

Brooch in the shape of a hand and wreath

MOURNING JEWELRY
When a member of a family died, close relatives would go into mourning for a period, wearing dark and somber clothes. All elaborate jewelry would be put away, and mourning jewelry would be worn. Mourning etiquette was religiously observed by all classes of society, and the demand for this jewelry was so great that it had to be mass-produced.

HOME MAID
Maids were employed in many households. Despite having to work very long and arduous hours, the fashion-conscious maid would have to spend some of her spare time sewing her own clothes. She would almost certainly have made her own version of the hooped crinoline petticoat.

WATCH AND CHAIN
In the 19th century, gentlemen wore a great deal of jewelry in the form of watches, watch-chains with fobs, or ornaments, tie pins, and rings. This gold pocket watch with chain and fob is typical of the period.

Fob is engraved in the style of a gold locket

EARLY AUTOMATION
Some of the first sewing machines were destroyed by mobs who thought their jobs were being threatened by automation. In fact, the sewing machine created a whole new industry that provided more work for everybody.

THE SOMBER MAN
The dress of the 19th-century gentleman became almost a uniform. By the early 1850s, almost all men wore black, navy, or dark gray frock coats with checked, plaid, or striped trousers, and vests that provided the only real color. This reproduction costume features a double-breasted vest with a single-breasted frock coat. Toward 1860, striped tartan and loud checks became the favored style for vests.

Side-whiskers were fashionable for men

Cravat

Vest provided dash of color

THE DEMURE LADY
This original dress of the late 1850s is typical of the middle classes. The two-piece dress is of floral silk brocade with black-silk fringing and black-velvet trimming. The elbow-length sleeves have undersleeves which could be taken out for cleaning, and the bodice is trimmed with small gilt buttons. By this time, the dress was supported by a crinoline (pp. 42–43) and several petticoats.

Detachable undersleeves

Black silk or net mittens were worn indoors during the day

Frock coat

Dress is made of silk

PANTALOONS
Girls wore dresses supported by full petticoats. It was also customary for girls to wear pantaloons (long drawers, or underwear).

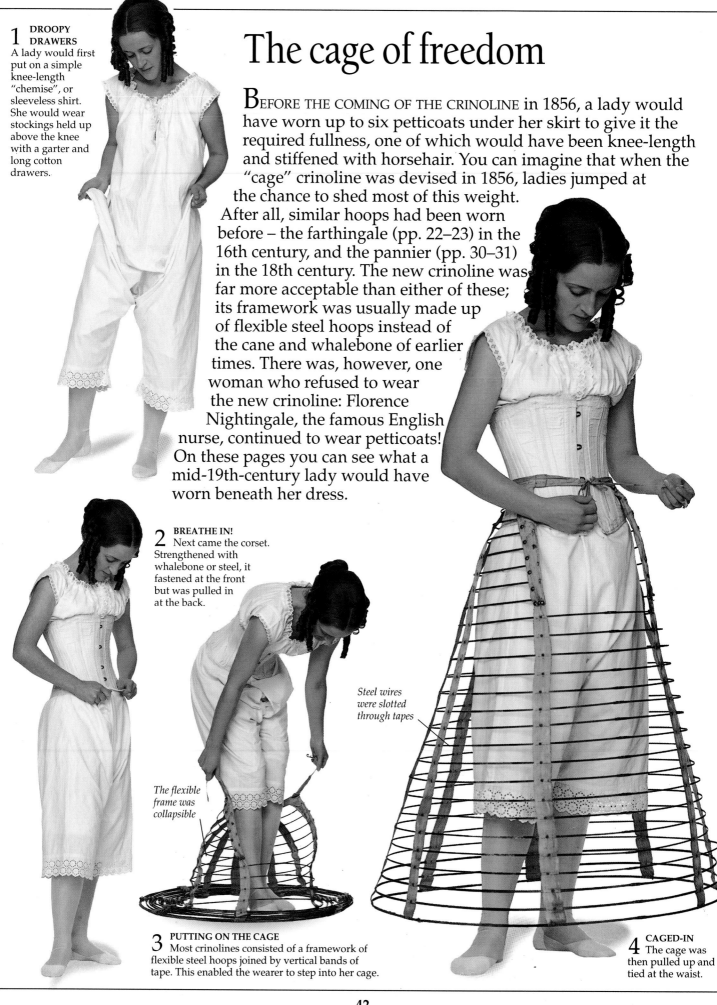

1 DROOPY DRAWERS

A lady would first put on a simple knee-length "chemise", or sleeveless shirt. She would wear stockings held up above the knee with a garter and long cotton drawers.

The cage of freedom

BEFORE THE COMING OF THE CRINOLINE in 1856, a lady would have worn up to six petticoats under her skirt to give it the required fullness, one of which would have been knee-length and stiffened with horsehair. You can imagine that when the "cage" crinoline was devised in 1856, ladies jumped at the chance to shed most of this weight. After all, similar hoops had been worn before – the farthingale (pp. 22–23) in the 16th century, and the pannier (pp. 30–31) in the 18th century. The new crinoline was far more acceptable than either of these; its framework was usually made up of flexible steel hoops instead of the cane and whalebone of earlier times. There was, however, one woman who refused to wear the new crinoline: Florence Nightingale, the famous English nurse, continued to wear petticoats! On these pages you can see what a mid-19th-century lady would have worn beneath her dress.

2 BREATHE IN!

Next came the corset. Strengthened with whalebone or steel, it fastened at the front but was pulled in at the back.

Steel wires were slotted through tapes

The flexible frame was collapsible

3 PUTTING ON THE CAGE

Most crinolines consisted of a framework of flexible steel hoops joined by vertical bands of tape. This enabled the wearer to step into her cage.

4 CAGED-IN

The cage was then pulled up and tied at the waist.

5 PRETTY PETTICOAT

The crinoline cage was then covered with a petticoat, which could be quite simple or elaborately trimmed with tucks, embroidery, and lace. Most petticoats were made of white cotton.

SHIP AHOY!
As crinolines became ever larger, it became impossible for two ladies to walk through a door together or to sit on the same sofa. It was also difficult for a lady's escort to get anywhere near her!

RADICAL BLOOMERS
In 1851, Mrs. Amelia Bloomer, an American, tried to introduce baggy, ankle-length trousers to replace wide skirts. She was ridiculed at the time, but bloomers were adopted for cycling nearly 50 years later.

6 MORE PETTICOATS

The number of petticoats worn with a crinoline depended on the size of the cage and the dress, but it was usually two.

7 THE FINISHED LOOK

This mid-19th-century dress completes the dressing. It is strange to think that this demure look was achieved by such a mass of cotton, lace, whalebone, and steel. Imagine having to put all this on in the morning when you are running late!

Dress is made of silk

Blushing brides

ALTHOUGH THE TRADITIONAL "white wedding" dates from the 19th century, the idea of wearing white as a symbol of purity has existed for about 400 years. Typically, all-white outfits are worn by babies, young children, and "innocent" victims in literature. Before the 19th century, the bride and bridegroom generally wore garments that were fashionable at the time, but of a better quality and more elaborate than their usual wear.

A SOLEMN AFFAIR
No specific color was worn at weddings in the Middle Ages. The style and richness of dress depended on the wealth of the couple. Note the elaborate headwear so typical of the period (pp. 14–15).

THE BRIDE WORE CREAM
The wedding dress of a mid-19th-century bride varied only slightly from her everyday clothes, and would have been worn as her "best" after the wedding. This original 1840s dress is in cream silk. A bonnet, mittens, and small purse complete the look.

CHASTE AND FERTILE
These wedding accessories belonged to a bride of 1889. The veil, gloves, posy, handkerchief, and ribbons appear almost as they were worn more than 100 years ago. The wax orange-blossom head-dress (below) from the same wedding, was a symbol of chastity and fertility.

Veil

Ribbons

Wax orange blossom headdress

The wearing of orange blossoms at weddings originated in France, from where it spread to North America and Britain

SIGNING THE REGISTER
In this late 19th-century painting by James Charles, you can see the bride, who is surrounded by her family and friends, signing the wedding register.

BEAMING BRIDE
This bridal dress was made for a wedding in 1925, then carefully stored with all of its accessories. The dress, in cream-silk satin crepe, has the short, wrapover-style skirt so fashionable in the mid-1920s. A "chaplet", or band, of wax orange blossoms holds the silk veil in place just above the eyes. You can see the real bride and groom in the wedding photograph at the bottom of this page.

Orange-blossoms band

Sleeves are bound with satin

Wrapover skirt

EAST MEETS WEST
It is not unusual today to find white weddings taking place all over the world. The adoption of Western-style marriage cere-monies and fashions is common with many young Asian people, who are keen to west-ernize every aspect of their daily lives.

ROMANTIC ROSES
Roses are the essence of romance and have become very popular for weddings. This bridesmaid's head-band was worn in 1971, and the bridal bouquet carried in 1985.

ROYAL WEDDING
Throughout history, royal weddings have had a potent fairy-tale quality, which the public enjoys immensely. When the former actress Grace Kelly married Prince Rainier in Monaco in 1956, the eyes of the world were upon them. The bride wore a full-skirted silk-and-lace wedding dress with a handmade lace veil. The veil was sewn with small seed pearls, and the fitted bodice was buttoned down the front with cultured pearls.

PRETTY PETTICOAT
This handmade silk petticoat was worn underneath the wedding dress on the left, and was almost certainly made by the bride herself or by her mother. The yoke is crocheted, and pearls have been sewn around the sleeves.

Handy hats

HAT OF ROSES
This straw hat of 1918 typifies the halfway stage between the large, fancy hat of the early 20th century (pp. 50–51) and the simpler 1920s "cloche" (bottom right).

Hats have been worn by men and women, through all ages, and in all parts of the world. Although originally worn mainly to provide protection from the weather and to indicate the status of the wearer, hats went on to become an important fashion accessory in their own right. In Europe, men have worn hats from classical times onward, but women rarely wore hats until the end of the 16th century. The large wigs of the mid-18th century (pp. 32–33) made the wearing of hats impractical for men, but they were often carried under the arm. Women still managed to balance a hat on top of their towering wigs! Toward the end of the 19th and beginning of the 20th centuries, many hats were very elaborate (pp. 50–51), and respectable men and women were never seen out without one. It was even known for top hats to be worn for gardening!

SMOKING CAP
Smoking caps were worn by many 19th-century gentlemen while relaxing at home. They were generally pillbox-shaped and often embroidered and trimmed with a tassel (pp. 36–37).

STRAW BOATER
Although originally worn by men for river boating and at the seaside, the boater was later adopted by young women.

ALL AROUND THE STEEPLES
High steeple, or "hennin," headdresses were typical of the 15th century (pp. 14–15). The very tall version was worn mainly in France, while the English favored the shorter "flowerpot" style.

WIG OR HAT?
This mid-1920s "wig" hat is of coarse gold thread and styled with braided "earphones."

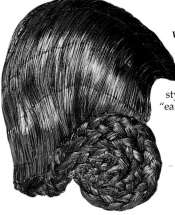

ANYONE FOR OPERA?
The collapsible opera hat was made of black silk stretched over a collapsible steel frame. This allowed the wearer to fold it so that it would go under his seat at the opera house or theater.

19th-century opera hat

FINE BONNET
This fancy 19th-century bonnet would have been worn on the back of the head. It is decorated with fine silk net, lace, fabric roses, a pink velvet ribbon, and a cream-colored feather.

HOOPED BONNET
Cane hoops help to keep this 19th-century child's hat in shape.

HIGH HATS
Headdresses reached their most extreme during the 18th century. This did not prevent ladies from wearing a hat perched on top!

RIDING BOWLER
This brown riding bowler has a ring on the brim to which a cord was attached to stop the hat from falling off when in full gallop.

Ring

BLACK STRAW
This stylish black straw hat from the 1940s is decorated with pressed flowers.

BROWN VELOUR
This woman's felt hat dates from the 1930s.

Silk leaves

TO WEAR OR EAT?
Red glass beads make this 1950s summer "berry" hat look almost good enough to eat – especially to birds!

Silk velvet petals

ANYONE FOR DARTS?
The success of British milliner, or hat designer and maker, David Shilling is partly due to the publicity his mother created when she wore his outlandish hats to the Ascot races.

FINE FEATHERS
In the early 18th and late 19th centuries, hats were great concoctions of lace, ribbon, flowers, and feathers. Ostrich feathers in particular were much sought after.

SILK HAT
The shape of this fine silk hat from the 1920s is maintained by a wire-frame base.

Brim of openwork pattern

Early 20th-century sporting gentleman

TOP HAT
Top hats varied greatly in shape and height. This one is thought to be a 19th-century coachman's hat.

WHERE'S MY HORSE?
Riding hats were specially strengthened to protect the rider's head. The top hat was popular with both men and women – the latter often adding a veil.

CLOCHE
The universal "cloche" hat of the 1920s covered the whole head and ears very tightly, making it almost impossible to have long hair.

Feathers and lace

BEARDS AND MUSTACHES
The beards and mustaches so popular during the early 1900s needed daily attention to keep them waxed and trimmed.

I<small>N</small> E<small>NGLAND IT WAS KNOWN AS</small> "the Edwardian era," and in France it was *"la belle époque."* In both countries, the early years of the 20th century were full of change, travel, and excitement. While rich women flocked to Paris to buy the latest fashions, some of the many poor scraped together enough money to emigrate to the U.S.A. – the "land of opportunity." Once there, they became the backbone of the garment-making sweatshops of New York City that supplied the fashion industry. While the upper classes floated about in a froth of feathers, lace, and pearls, the middle-class working girl earned her living in simple tailored clothes, doubtless dreaming of Charles Dana Gibson's drawings of the American Langhorne sisters, who became known as the Gibson Girls. These sisters typified the glamour of the age, and their image was familiar all over the world.

STROLLING AND SHOPPING
The luxurious department stores of the time attracted a daily gathering of elegant women eager to display their wealth through the latest fashions.

SEPARATE SLEEVES
Sleeves were often sold separately. These lace sleeves are similar to the sleeves of the blue dress on the next page. It is likely they were purchased for future use, but never used.

Ten rows of pearls held by silver bars make up this choker necklace

Silver necklace set with amethysts, seed pearls, and green garnets in its original case

PEARLS
To complement the delicate evening wear of the time, jewelry was suitably fine. Necklaces such as these were worn, pearls being the favorite choice. Jewelry featuring insects and flowers was also popular.

AND SO TO BED
When the expensive handmade lace (pp. 50–51) was replaced with the cheaper machine-made product, lace was used for many items of clothing – such as this bed jacket.

THE SMART SET
Much of early 20th-century smart society spent winters in Monte Carlo and other Mediterranean resorts.

FANTASTIC FAN
Evening fans were large and opulent, often made of silk or feathers. This embroidered silk fan decorated with tiny spangles is typical of the period.

Ivory frame

THE "S"- SHAPE
Corsets of the early 1900s were designed to force the bust forward and thrust the hips back. The overall effect was of a large bust, tiny waist, and pronounced derriere! This look is known as the "S"-shape.

RIGID GRACE
These Gibson Girl-style ladies appeared in a 1907 fashion illustration and typify the extravagant evening wear and contorted "S"-shape of the early 1900s.
Lingerie-type fabrics and yards of billowing lace ruffles were much in evidence. Because a different outfit was required for each occasion, the society woman changed her clothes several times a day.

A simpler line

THE SECOND DECADE of the 20th century saw a change in the female figure. It became more upright, and soft materials were replaced with more substantial fabrics. For men, the black morning coat replaced the frock coat, so popular for formal daywear in the 19th century (pp. 40–41). The biggest change in menswear came with the lounge suit, which consisted of a shorter jacket, vest, and trousers in matching fabric. It was often worn with a homburg hat.

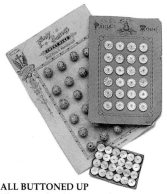

HOBBLE SKIRTS
Skirts became increasingly narrow at the hem from about 1910. Some became so narrow that women could only hobble about with tiny steps.

ALL BUTTONED UP
These cards of buttons date from the early 1900s. The larger cards hold white cotton-covered underwear buttons, and the smaller cards hold mother-of-pearl buttons used for shirts and blouses.

FREEDOM FOR WOMEN!
The women's emancipation movement of the early 20th century led to the freedom of women from many constraints and also won them the right to vote. Women were able to join in sports and other "masculine" activities, as the uncomfortable corset gradually disappeared and skirts became looser and less restrictive.

RACE DAY
The morning suit and topper were "common" dress for gentlemen spending the day at the races.

Cream-colored lace blouse of 1906

FANCY KNICKERS
These silk "skirt knickers" date from around 1908. Plain cotton drawers are attached to an elaborate taffeta and lace petticoat.

This detail shows the lace pattern and silk-covered buttons used to decorate the blouse

BEAUTIFUL BLOUSES
Lace blouses were an extremely important part of a lady's wardrobe in the early 20th century. They were worn with a plain skirt, or with one of the tailored two-piece suits so popular for day wear.

TOP-HEAVY
This early 20th-century straw hat is laden with silk flowers and foliage. As skirts became narrower, hats became larger and were considered so important that women wore them even in their own homes.

EVENING ELEGANCE
Evening bags were as elaborate as the dresses, as seen by this blue-and-gold example from about 1900.

HAT BITS
Pure silk ribbons and other hand-made trimmings like these were used by milliners to decorate new hats – or to revive old ones.

GLADSTONE BAG
This slim leather Gladstone-style day handbag was very popular with the tailored look of 1910.

FINE FEATHERS
To satisfy the enormous world-wide demand for the feathers so necessary for hats, fans, and boas (feather scarves) of the time, ostrich farms became an overnight industry.

Mauve ostrich-feather boa of around 1905

SLIMMER AND SIMPLER
The rigid bodices and bell-shaped skirts so popular earlier in the decade (pp. 48–49) gave way to a much slimmer line introduced in Paris around 1910 – as shown by this pale-blue linen dress of around 1911.

Crocheted details

WATCH THAT ANKLE!
The buttoned boot continued to be the favorite outdoor footwear. This slim boot with its Louis heel (first worn by Louis XV of France, who reigned from 1715–1774) enabled ladies to "show" their shapely ankles.

A new world

ALTHOUGH WORLD WAR I (1914–1918) and its aftermath brought disillusionment and unrest, the younger generation was determined to start "a fresh world." Perhaps the greatest change in fashion came with the new, softer undergarments. Indeed, it was said that the discarding of the whalebone corset did as much for women's emancipation as did getting the vote. Work, sports, dancing, the automobile, and American movies all left their mark on fashion. The 1920s and 1930s will best be remembered as the era of Gabrielle (Coco) Chanel, whose simpler lines led to the flat-chested look of the 1920s, and Elsa Schiaparelli, credited with the sinuous line and padded shoulders of the 1930s.

Chanel glass necklace of 1930

THE SPORTY TYPE
This 1920s checked three-piece suit was considered sportswear, and would never have been worn in town. It is worn on the right with a wide-sectioned country cap.

TWOS OR FOURS?
These wide knicker-bockers are known as plus-twos; wider, longer versions are known as plus-fours – perhaps referring to the extra fabric needed to make them.

ONE COLD DRINK, PLEASE
The loose-fitting trousers that some very fashionable women wore in the 1920s were known as beach or lounging pajamas. This beach outfit is from the summer of 1929.

LONG AND STRAIGHT
The silhouette of the early 1920s woman was long and straight, as shown by these American fashion drawings of 1924. The bust has been flattened, the natural waist ignored, and the belt lowered to the hip.

ART SILK TO RAYON
The 1920s sweater on the left has bands of crocheting and knitting, and the one on the right is hand-knitted. Both are made of art silk, which later became known as rayon.

NO POCKETS
To complement the slinky evening gowns of the 1930s, evening bags became an essential item. Such clinging creations as these gowns left no room for unsightly pockets.

CLINGING CREPE
The strongest impact on women's clothes was the bias cut – cutting a garment diagonally across the fabric – which allowed the dress to cling to the body. Gone was the short, flat-chested, low-waisted look of the boyish 1920s!

WAVES AND CURLS
"Marcels," permanent curls or waves, were introduced in 1920 and remained popular through-out the 1930s.

OXFORD BAGS
In 1925, the wide-legged baggy trousers that originated among Oxford undergraduates in England became fashionable on both sides of the Atlantic, and became known as "Oxford bags." Although the fashion lasted only a short time, it has been revived in other guises over the decades.

CAREFREE FLAPPERS
The popular, bouncy dances of the 1920s inspired the use of fringes and beads to emphasize the movement of the dancers, known as flappers. Joan Crawford (above) became known as the "all-American Charleston-dancing flapper."

MAKE MINE WOOL
In the 1920s and 1930s the sweater became an alternative to the blouse. This simple 1930s sweater was hand-knitted. The buttons are typical of the period.

STRONG STYLE
These fashionable scarves from the 1920s and 1930s in silk or rayon are printed in bold stylized designs popular at the time.

Fashion foundations

"PULL HARDER!"
Sometimes the corset had to be ferociously tight-laced in order to achieve the desired small waist. This was often achieved with much breath-holding on the part of the lady concerned, and a great deal of exhaustion on the part of her helpers!

Aᴌᴛʜᴏᴜɢʜ ᴜɴᴅᴇʀᴡᴇᴀʀ has always been worn by both men and women for reasons of warmth and hygiene, each new fashion era has called for its own foundation garments. Indeed, there have been few times in the history of costume when the female form has not been laced in or padded out – from the bust flatteners of the 1920s and the padded brassières of the 1950s, to the farthingales of the 16th century (pp. 22–23) and the crinolines of the 19th century (pp.40–43). Materials as diverse as whalebone, steel, horsehair, and elastic have all been used to achieve the required shape.

Woolen corset from the 1890s

WOOL NEXT TO THE SKIN
Nineteenth-century corsets were considered unhygienic. To remedy this, Dr. Jaeger of Germany promoted the wearing of wool next to the skin, and from 1884 woolen corsets like this were made.

BULKY BUSTLES
Various artificial supports have been worn through the centuries for supporting skirts, but were most widely used in the second half of the 19th century. The bustle replaced the crinoline (pp. 40–43), and although it went out of fashion at the end of the 1870s, it returned in 1882. Bustles varied greatly in style and length.

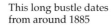

This long bustle dates from around 1885

SILENT AGONY
Between the 1880s and 1905, corsets like this one were at their most rigid and agonizing. They were very long and restricting at the waist, and it was not unknown for ladies of the time to suffer broken ribs and displaced vital organs!

LACE AND LAWN
Corset covers and camisoles were worn over the corset in the mid-to late 19th century to stop the corset from rubbing against the dress. At first they were quite simple, but as they came into the 20th century they became much prettier, with lace insertions and frills. Often these lawn and lace creations were woven through with silk ribbons.

Early 20th-century camisole

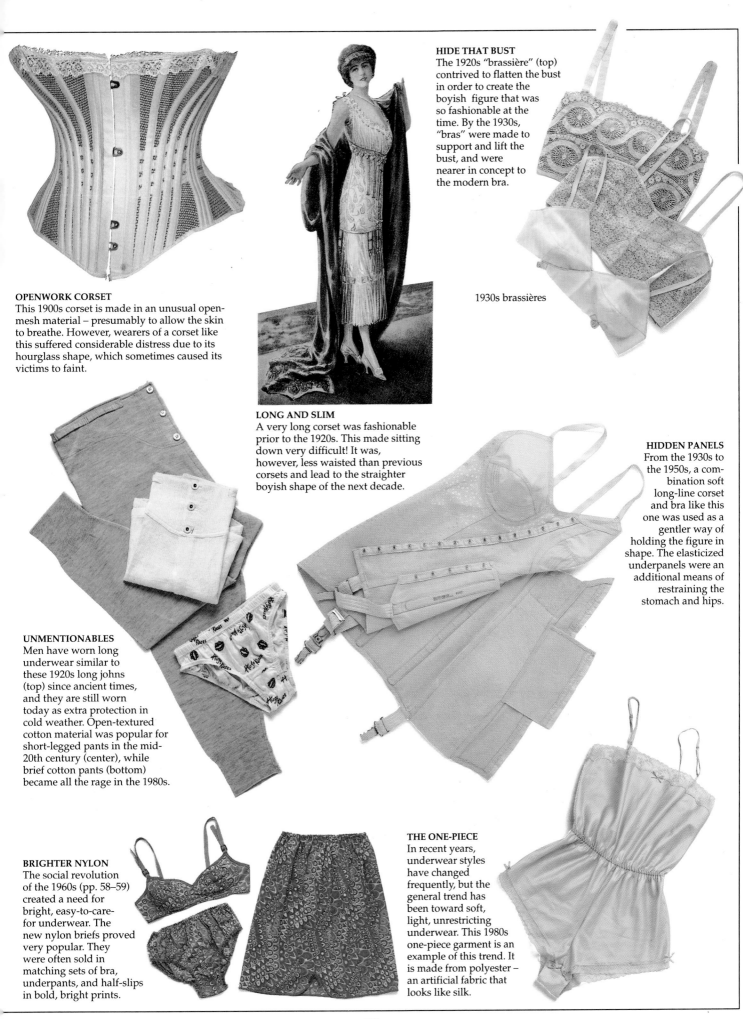

OPENWORK CORSET
This 1900s corset is made in an unusual open-mesh material – presumably to allow the skin to breathe. However, wearers of a corset like this suffered considerable distress due to its hourglass shape, which sometimes caused its victims to faint.

HIDE THAT BUST
The 1920s "brassière" (top) contrived to flatten the bust in order to create the boyish figure that was so fashionable at the time. By the 1930s, "bras" were made to support and lift the bust, and were nearer in concept to the modern bra.

1930s brassières

LONG AND SLIM
A very long corset was fashionable prior to the 1920s. This made sitting down very difficult! It was, however, less waisted than previous corsets and lead to the straighter boyish shape of the next decade.

HIDDEN PANELS
From the 1930s to the 1950s, a combination soft long-line corset and bra like this one was used as a gentler way of holding the figure in shape. The elasticized underpanels were an additional means of restraining the stomach and hips.

UNMENTIONABLES
Men have worn long underwear similar to these 1920s long johns (top) since ancient times, and they are still worn today as extra protection in cold weather. Open-textured cotton material was popular for short-legged pants in the mid-20th century (center), while brief cotton pants (bottom) became all the rage in the 1980s.

BRIGHTER NYLON
The social revolution of the 1960s (pp. 58–59) created a need for bright, easy-to-care-for underwear. The new nylon briefs proved very popular. They were often sold in matching sets of bra, underpants, and half-slips in bold, bright prints.

THE ONE-PIECE
In recent years, underwear styles have changed frequently, but the general trend has been toward soft, light, unrestricting underwear. This 1980s one-piece garment is an example of this trend. It is made from polyester – an artificial fabric that looks like silk.

Before and after

CLOTHING WAS STRICTLY controlled during World War II (1939–1945); materials were scarce, and many workers from the fashion industry were transferred into war-related industries. Clothes were designed to be hard-wearing and functional, and were mostly styled into short, boxy shapes. After the war, in 1947, the Parisian fashion designer Christian Dior launched a dramatic change of fashion known as the New Look– tightly fitting corseted bodices and long, full skirts, often worn with narrow high heels. This style dominated fashion for the remainder of the 1940s and 1950s, although from the late 1940s, teenagers – who were increasingly under the influence of American pop and film stars – began to wear different clothes from those of their parents.

1940s Pierot costume jewelery

LEAN AND LONG
Dior's New Look was so glamorous that it was immediately copied by other designers. This early 1950s suit is cut in the style of the New Look, but the skirt does not have the same quantities of fabric and is not as full as Dior's original styles.

CHERRY BROOCH
During the war, some women made their own jewelry from everyday items such as corks and bottle tops. Cheap plastic jewelry, like this brooch, was also sold in stores.

UTILITY WEAR
Wartime shortages resulted in the "Utility" scheme in Britain. A standard outfit for women was a little hat, square padded shoulders, knee-length skirt, and sensible shoes, which often had wedge heels.

THE ARRIVAL OF NYLON
These 1940s seamed stockings are made of nylon, introduced during the war. Nylon was sheer, hard-wearing, and much cheaper than silk.

PRACTICAL WEDGES
These 1940s women's lace-up, wedge-sole shoes are made from reptile skin. The soles were often made from cork or wood.

Ankle-strap shoes were very fashionable at this time

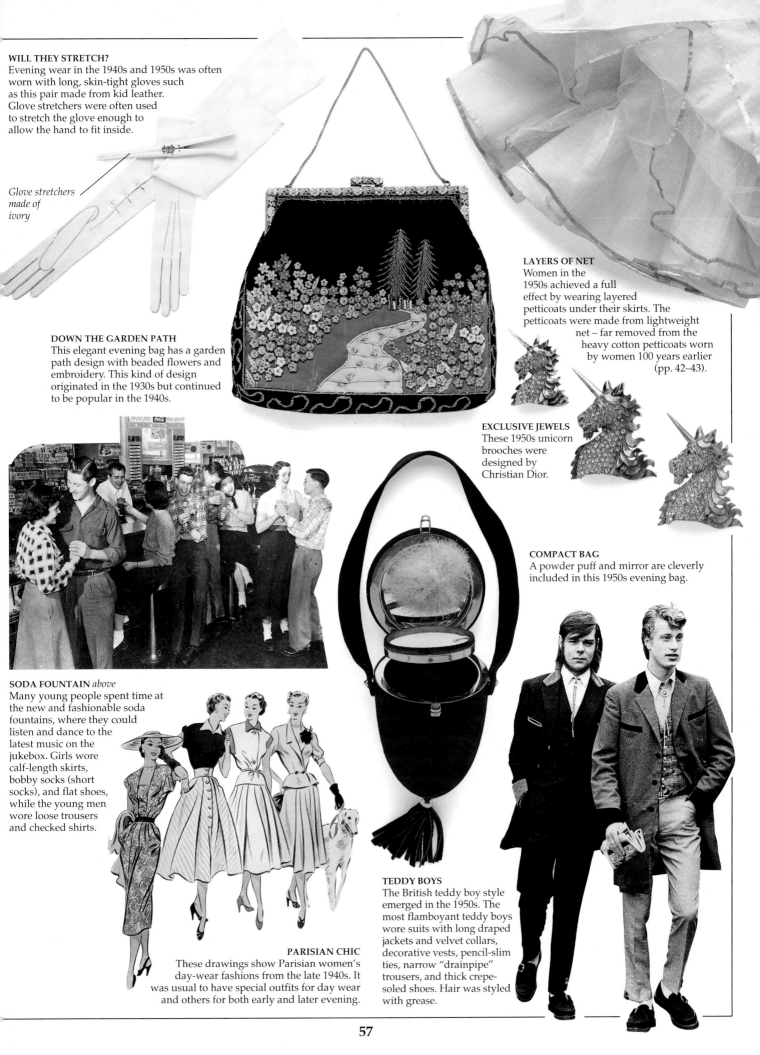

WILL THEY STRETCH?
Evening wear in the 1940s and 1950s was often worn with long, skin-tight gloves such as this pair made from kid leather. Glove stretchers were often used to stretch the glove enough to allow the hand to fit inside.

Glove stretchers made of ivory

DOWN THE GARDEN PATH
This elegant evening bag has a garden path design with beaded flowers and embroidery. This kind of design originated in the 1930s but continued to be popular in the 1940s.

LAYERS OF NET
Women in the 1950s achieved a full effect by wearing layered petticoats under their skirts. The petticoats were made from lightweight net – far removed from the heavy cotton petticoats worn by women 100 years earlier (pp. 42–43).

EXCLUSIVE JEWELS
These 1950s unicorn brooches were designed by Christian Dior.

COMPACT BAG
A powder puff and mirror are cleverly included in this 1950s evening bag.

SODA FOUNTAIN *above*
Many young people spent time at the new and fashionable soda fountains, where they could listen and dance to the latest music on the jukebox. Girls wore calf-length skirts, bobby socks (short socks), and flat shoes, while the young men wore loose trousers and checked shirts.

PARISIAN CHIC
These drawings show Parisian women's day-wear fashions from the late 1940s. It was usual to have special outfits for day wear and others for both early and later evening.

TEDDY BOYS
The British teddy boy style emerged in the 1950s. The most flamboyant teddy boys wore suits with long draped jackets and velvet collars, decorative vests, pencil-slim ties, narrow "drainpipe" trousers, and thick crepe-soled shoes. Hair was styled with grease.

Minis, boots, and bell-bottoms

THE MOST RECENT PERIOD of great diversity and change in fashion was in the 1960s, when new, daring styles were adopted by the young. This decade saw the introduction of clothes made from new and exciting materials such as shiny and see-through plastics, metals, and even paper, while fashions for women became shorter and more revealing than at any other time. In the late 1960s the hippy movement emerged and, in complete contrast, created a vogue for long, flowing garments in natural materials. Subsequent fashions used a combination of these styles until the distinctive punk style made its dramatic entrance around 1976.

KEEP CLEAN!
The look and texture of these transparent plastic 1960s dresses were very different than anything known before. They had to be wiped clean because they would have melted in a hot wash!

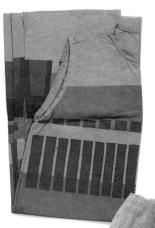

PAPER PANTS
Bright, contrasting colors and disposable clothes were high fashion in the 1960s. This folded dress and underpants were designed to be worn just once and then thrown away.

Poppit beads

Plastic earrings

CHUNKY PLASTIC
Many styles of jewelry were worn in the 1960s, including brightly colored plastic items. This necklace is made of poppit beads – they could be added on or taken off according to the length desired and were often worn by children for "dress-up."

MINI MADNESS
This high-waisted mini dress was designed by Ossie Clark in 1965. Although it looks like a child's dress, it was for an adult.

Black and gold metallic thread is woven through fabric

BOOTS ARE A MUST
Boots accompanied most outfits in the 1960s. This knee-length pair may have been worn with a matching coat or dress.

MINI MINI
The mini dress, with its mid-thigh-length skirt, became a symbol of the rebellious youth of the 1960s .

58

HAPPY HIPPIES
Hippies believed that clothes should express individuality and that fashion should not be dictated by a few select fashion designers. Hippies wore a great variety of styles and fabrics, largely inspired by fashions from around the world. These included sheepskin coats, caftans, heavy velvet clothes, fringed leather bags, African textiles, exotic beads, and flowing scarves. Many walked barefoot or wore strappy leather sandals. The most extreme dyed their hair bright colors and painted swirling flower designs on their faces and bodies.

Many male hippies wore beads

Vest has a flower motif

Beaded and fringed bag

Fabrics with optical effects were very fashionable

HOT-PANT SUIT
Hot-pants, introduced in the early 1970s, offered an alternative to the ever-popular miniskirt. They were worn by older children as well as adults.

This hot-pant suit belonged to an 11-year-old girl.

BELL-BOTTOMS
Both men and women wore bell-bottoms (wide-bottomed trousers) in the early1970s, and embroidered clothes were particularly popular. These trousers are decorated with a floral and butterfly design.

"Flower power" embroidery

Feet were visible through clear-plastic uppers

PLATFORMS
Platform shoes for both sexes were at their most fashionable and extreme in the 1970s.

HIPPIES HANG OUT
These hippies are at an open-air rock concert. Hippies wanted to break the traditional boundaries between men's and women's clothes. Many men grew their hair long and wore beads and pastel colors to express their views visually.

"SHOCKING" GEAR
The dyed and spiked hairstyles, slashed jeans, holey fishnet tights, heavy boots, and leather jackets worn by this couple are typical late 1970s punk style. Slashed clothes were first seen in the 16th century (pp. 20–21).

Boys and girls together

CHILDREN WORE the same style of clothes as their parents from the time of the ancient civilizations of Egypt, Greece, Rome, and Byzantium until the late 18th century. At that time, children's clothes began to have a style of their own, and their wearers ceased to look like miniature adults. From the early 19th century, these new styles were still very formal; the real revolution in children's clothes came after World War II, when they began to have the relaxed and casual look they have today.

BOY OR GIRL?
Believe it or not, this silk tartan dress from 1860 was worn by a boy. Small boys wore dresses and had long curly hair until they were about six years old.

WHITE FRILLS
This girl's coat and bonnet are from the early 20th century. Such a crisp, clean outfit would certainly not have been suitable for playing in the dirt!

Matching cap

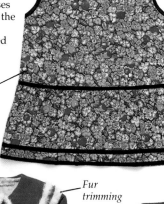

PRETTY PRINT
This girl's dress from the mid-1920s is similar to the adult dresses of the time. It has the same "Peter Pan" collar and dropped waistline.

Fabric is printed with a cherry and blossom pattern

Fur trimming

COAT AND LEGGINGS
Matching coats and leggings were popular around the 1930s and 1940s. The leggings zip tightly over the shoes for extra warmth.

LITTLE DANDY
This typical 1930s boy's double-breasted coat and matching cap is made of fine herringbone tweed. The coat is fastened with horn buttons.

Side opening

FANCY PANTS
This is a pair of 19th-century boy's cotton drawers.

THE "IN" LOOK
Today, the casual blue-jean-and-T-shirt look is "in" for both younger and older children. The style originated in the U.S.A. and was soon adopted all over the world.

CURLS AND SASHES
This detail is taken from a 1789 portrait by the English artist Sir Joshua Reynolds (1723–1792). You may well assume that it is of a little girl, but in fact it is of the son of a wealthy family of the period.

LONG AND FLOWING
The lines of this girl's dress follow those of the ladies' robes of the time – c. 1100 (pp. 14–15). She also wears her long hair in a braid.

CHILDREN AT PLAY
The clothes that these late 19th-century children are wearing do not seem very suitable for playing outside. The girls are even wearing fancy hats.

Bustle

Pantaloons

Shirt frill hints at the ruff which was to follow (pp. 20–21)

Hose

16TH CENTURY MEETS 19TH CENTURY
The little girl on the left is wearing an original red-wool bustle dress of the 1880s. The bustle is tied into shape with tapes inside. The boy on the right is wearing a reproduction costume that shows a typical outfit of the early 16th century.

Fashion design

FASHION HAS BECOME increasingly international during the second half of the 20th century – with Paris, New York, Milan, and London as the major fashion capitals. However, the market for "couture" clothing (custom made, or made-to-order, designs for select clients) has dwindled, and smaller companies producing original ready-to-wear clothes aimed at a younger market have sprung up. One such company is London-based Workers for Freedom. These pictures show the processes involved in making one of their unisex shirts.

THE DESIGN
Designer Richard Nott works on ideas for new garments for the spring/summer collection. The picture board to his left provides inspiration with its design ideas and swatches of fabrics that he selected in advance from the Paris trade shows.

FLOWERS AND STRIPES
The bold use of striped fabric and a floral design makes this Workers for Freedom suit daringly different.

DESIGN DETAILS
These detailed drawings show the design for the poplin unisex shirt featured on these pages and for a woman's embroidered jacket. The heavy curved design is one of several appliqué motifs used throughout the collection.

ON THE MACHINE
The machinist makes up the sample garment from the cut-out fabric. In this picture she is finishing off the buttonholes.

This trademark label is sewn into all Workers for Freedom garments.

PAPER PATTERN
Once the design is finished, a paper pattern is cut and the sample garment is made. If successful, the pattern shapes are then cut from cardboard.

FASHION SHOW
These photographs were taken at the fashion show attended by the international buyers and the press.

COLOR AND CONTRAST
These sample shirts were made up in three colors, all of which were used in the final collection.

SWIRLS AND DRAGONS
The flowing designs on this finished outfit harmonize well, although Workers for Freedom also combines angular and curvy designs with great success. Asian-influenced designs like the dragons used on these trousers have been particularly fashionable since the late 1980s.

ON THE RUNWAY
After much hard work, the collection is brought together to present to the press and clients. You can see the variety of garments produced for the season and the different ways they can be worn together.

PRODUCTION COSTS
Richard Nott and his partner – business manager Graham Fraser – discuss the production costs of the shirt in order to decide upon a final price.

ORDER SHEETS
These customer order sheets, with sketches and written descriptions of the collection, recall for the buyers, at a glance, the outfits they have seen on the runway. They help buyers to place their orders once the show has finished.

Index

A

accessories 18-19, 25, 27, 36, 39, 44
Anglo Saxon costume 12-13

B

baldric 27, 29
bathing clothes 34-35
beads 6, 18, 57, 58, 59
beauty patches 18, 32
bell-bottoms 59
belts 13, 14, 15, 27, 36
bikini 35
bloomers 24, 34, 37, 43
blouses 9, 50
boa, feather 51
boater 46
bonnet 44, 46, 60
boots 12, 19, 20, 24, 25, 26, 51, 58, 59
bow tie 37
bowler 47
bracelet 13, 18
braids 11, 14, 61
brassière 54-55
breeches 21, 23, 26, 31, 32
bridal dress 44-45
briefs 55
brocade 15, 17, 24, 30, 38, 40, 41
brooch 12, 13, 15, 18, 19, 40
buckle 13, 15, 18, 25, 27, 32
bustle 40, 54, 61

C

caftan 59
cameo 19, 40
camisole 54
canvas shoes 24
cap 13, 15, 28, 36, 38, 46, 52
cape 20, 27
cassock 29
cavalier costume 26
chain mail 12
chaps 39
chatelaine 38
checks 41, 57
chemise 42
children's clothes 19, 22, 27, 47, 60-61
chiton 9
cloak 7, 12, 13, 18, 21
cloche hat 46, 47
clog 30
cloth cap 13
coats 26, 29, 32, 33
codpiece 16
collars 26, 27, 57
corsets 38, 39, 42, 49, 50, 52, 54-55
cotton fabric 9, 38-39
court dress 30, 33
couture 40, 62
cravats 29, 32, 37, 40, 41
crepe 45
crepe-soled shoes 57
crinolines 38, 40, 41, 42-43, 54
cuffs 8, 18, 28, 29, 30, 31

D

damask 17
doublet 16, 20, 21, 23
drainpipe trousers 57
drawers 35, 41, 42, 50, 60
dresses 8, 10, 16, 17, 18, 38
dyes 9, 11, 13, 23

E

Edwardian Era 48-49
Egyptian clothes 8, 9, 36, 60
elastic 35, 54, 55
European fashion 10, 12, 20, 26
evening bags 51, 53, 57

F

fabrics 14, 15, 16
fans 19, 27, 32, 39, 49, 51
farthingale 22, 23, 42, 54
fashion houses 40
felt 21
fichu 31
fishnet tights 59
flappers 53
flax 7, 8
fob 40
fontanges 28
footwear 24-25
French fashion 14, 20, 26, 28, 31
frock coats 39, 41, 50
fur 6, 7, 12, 13, 15, 16, 39

G

gaiters 37
garters 36, 37, 42
girdle 13, 15
Gladstone bag 51
gloves 19, 21, 27, 39, 44, 57
gold threads 11, 16, 17, 21
gowns 12, 16, 30, 38
Greek dress 8, 9, 18, 34, 60
guimpe 14

H

hairstyles 8, 10-11, 14, 18, 26, 28-29, 33, 59
handbag 31, 36, 39
handkerchief 18, 39, 44
hats 46-47
headdresses 14, 23, 44, 46, 47
helmet 9, 12, 13
high-heeled shoes 27, 36, 51
hippies 6, 58-59
hobble skirts 50
homburg hat 50
hooped skirts 42
hose 16, 17, 22
hot-pants 59
houppelande 16, 23

I

Italian fashion 14, 16-17, 19, 20, 23

J

jacket 23, 28, 29, 50, 57
jeans 59, 60
jerkin 20, 26
jewelry 16, 18, 36, 40, 48, 56, 58

K

kidskin 24, 32, 39, 57
knickerbockers 22, 23, 52
knickers 36, 50,

L

lawn 31, 54
linen 8, 9, 10, 12, 14, 28, 51
loincloths 8
long johns 55
lorgnettes 36
lounge suit 50

M

mantua gown 30
metal clothes 58
Middle Age fashions 14-15
mini dress 58
mittens 12, 19, 41, 44
mob cap 35
morning suit 50
mourning wear 28, 40
mules 25
muslin 18, 28, 31

N

necklace 6, 18, 48, 58
necktie 37
nightgown 12
nylon 55, 56

O

ostrich feathers 47, 51
overshoes 38
Oxford bags 53

P

pajamas 52
panniers 30, 42
pantaloons 41
paper clothes 58
parasols 19
patchboxes 18
pearls 11, 45, 48
peasecod belly 20, 21
peplos 9
periwigs 28, 29
pince-nez 36
plastic 36, 56, 58
platform shoes 24, 25, 59
plus-fours 52
plus-twos 52
polonaise dress 30
polyester 55
poulaines 24
powdered wigs 32
pumps 25
punk rockers 6, 58, 59
Puritan dress 27

R

rayon 52, 53
Renaissance clothes 16-17
reptile skin 24, 56
reticules 39
riding hat 47
Roman costume 10, 12, 18, 34, 60
ruffs 16, 18, 20, 21, 22, 26, 61

S

sandals 8, 10, 59
satin 24, 25, 45
scarves 9, 53, 59
shawls 7, 10, 39
shirt 12, 16, 21, 26, 57, 61
silk industry 11
silver threads 11, 17
slashed clothes 17, 20, 21, 59
slippers 11
smoking cap 36, 46
snuffboxes 18, 36
socks 57
spectacles 36
spinning 7, 8, 13, 14
stockings 12, 19, 31, 32, 37, 42, 56
stomachers 22, 30
straw hat 46, 47, 51
suede shoes 24, 25
suit 29, 50, 52, 56, 57
sunglasses 34, 36
surcoat 15
suspender 37
sweater 53
swimwear 34

T

tartan 41, 60
teddy boys 6, 57
templers 14
textiles 13
tiaras 11
tie 37, 40, 57
tights 16, 59
toga 10, 34
top hat 39, 46, 47
tricorn hat 28
trunk hose 22, 23
T-shirt 60
tweed 60

U

umbrellas 19, 37
underclothes 42-43, 52, 54-55
undercoat 15

V

veils 14, 44, 47
vests 28, 31, 33, 41, 50, 59
Viking costume 12-13, 18

W

walking stick 29, 36, 37
weaving 7, 8, 13, 14, 38
wedding dress 44-45
wedge-sole shoes 56
whalebone 20, 22, 23, 42, 52, 54
wigs 8, 11, 18, 28, 31, 32, 33, 38, 46
woolen cloth 7, 8

Acknowledgments

Dorling Kindersley would like to thank:
Vicky Davenport for editorial assistance; the Worthing Museum and Art Gallery; the Museum of London; the British Museum; Bermans and Nathans International Ltd; Cosprop Ltd; Sheila and Alan Buckland; Alan and Vanessa Hopkins; Harry Matthews; Workers for Freedom; Wig Specialities Ltd; Ray Marston Wigs; Siegel and Stockman; Helena Spiteri; Katie Martin. Special thanks to Duncan Brown, Christopher Davis, Sophie Mitchell, Christopher Howson, Sarah Ponder, Clifford Rosney, Christian Sévigny, Martin Atcherley, Richard Clemson, Helen Senior, Deborah Murrell, Anna Kunst, Céline Carez, Claire Gillard, Kirsty Burns, Christiane Gunzi, Holly Jackson, Paul Cannings, Jean-Michel Vivier, André and Desmond Brown for modeling the costumes and Jane Parker for the index.

Picture credits
t=top, b=bottom, c=center, l=left,

Advertising Archives: 25cr; Heather Angel: 7tr; Barnaby's Picture Library: 9br, 13br, 22tr, 37bl, 53tl, 58br; Bettman Archive: 57cl; Bridgeman Art Library: London: Bibliothèque Nationale, Paris: 14cl;/British Library, London: 16cr/ British Museum, London: 8tl/Musée Carnavalet, Paris 40cl; Christie's, London 27cl/ Musée Condé, Chantilly: 20tl/ Geffrye Museum, London: 40bl/Johnny Van Haeften Gallery, London: 29bc/ Private Collection: 39bl/Whitford & Hughes, London: 48br; British Museum: 14c; Chris Moore: 62tr, 62bl, 63tr; e.t. Archive 15cl, 16cr, 23ct, 23tr, 33tc, 33c, 38tl, 38cl, 44tr, 44bc, 48cl, 50c; Mary Evans Picture Library: 6cr, 6br, 7tl, 11tl, 12cl, 14tl, 24cr, 25cr, 28tl, 28cr, 32cr, 34cl, 36bc, 39tc, 42, 43, 46cl, 47cr, 47cl, 47bc, 50tl, 51cl, 53cl, 55tc, 61tl, 61cl; Michael Holford: 7b, 17tr; The Hulton Picture Company: 13cl, 19tl, 23cl, 58tl; Image Bank: 7cr, 35cl, 45tc; Imperial War Museum: 56cl; Kobal Collection: 53cr; Mansell Collection: 6tl, 11b, 12bl, 13tc, 15tc, 15bl, 21c, 22tl, 27tl, 30tl, 31cl, 39tl, 49; National Gallery: 21tc, 21tr, 23tl, 26r; National Portrait Gallery: 221; Peter Newark's Pictures: 7tc, 16tl, 16tr, 20bl, 23br, 26tl, 37cl, 48tl, 57bl; Robert Opie Collection: 60tc; Rex Features: 47cr, 59br; Sygma Ltd: 45c; The Telegraph Colour Library: 59bl; Frederick Warne & Co: 18tl; Worthing Museum and Art Gallery: 18tr, 18cr, 18bl, 19cr, 19bl, 19br, 27tr, 30tr, 30cr, 30br, 31tr, 31bl, 31bc, 2bl, 3cr, 3br, 5tr, 35tc, 35br, 36c, 36bl, 36br, 37tl, 37tr, 37cl, 37c, 37bc, 39tr, 39cr, 44cr, 45cr, 51tl, 51cl, 52br, 53tl, 55cl,55bl, 55br, 56tr, 58cl, 58c, 59tr, 59cr.

Hair and makeup:
Jenny Shircore
Louise Fisher

Additional Photography:
Steve Gorton
Torla Evans and John Chase of the Museum of London